Writers' Favorite Recipes

Writers' Favorite Recipes

Gillian Vincent

St. Martin's Press
New York

St. Martin's Press, Inc. 175 Fifth Ave., New York, N.Y. 10010
Manufactured in the United States of America

Library of Congress Cataloging in Publication Data

Main entry under title:

Writers' favorite recipes.

1. Cookery, British. 2. Cookery, International.
3. Authors, English. I. Vincent, Gillian.
TX717.W765 1980 641.5 79-5328
ISBN 0-312-89431-7

THE ILLUSTRATIONS

'Carving Instructions' from Eliza Acton's *Modern Cookery For Private Families* (Elek, 1966)
'Show Your Hands, Daisy' from E. Nesbit's *Long Ago When I Was Young* (Macdonald and Jane's, 1975)
'Serving champagne peaches' by Anton, from Desmond Briggs' *Entertaining Single-Handed* (Penguin, 1968)
'George Bernard Shaw Eating Letters' from *The George Bernard Shaw Vegetarian Cook Book* by courtesy of the Garnstone Press Ltd.
Quentin Blake's drawing of tea-time from Patrick Campbell's *Rough Husbandry* (Hutchinson, 1965)
Frank Dickens' cartoon from *More Bristow* (Beaverbrook Newspapers/Abelard Schuman, 1973)
'Max' from Giovannetti's *New Max Book* (Atheneum Publishers, New York, 1976) Pont cartoons from Bernard Hollowood's book *Pont: The Life and Work of the Great Punch Cartoonist*, (Collins, 1969)
'An Improved Dinner Wagon' by kind permission of Oliver Robinson
'How To Roast Lamb' from Willie Rushton's *Superpig* (Macdonald and Jane's, 1976)
'Some English Jam Tart Designs' from Dorothy Hartley's *Food in England* (Macdonald and Jane's, 1975)

PREFACE

This book is fun; it is (or at least can be) useful; and every copy sold benefits an organisation whose aims are particularly worthy in a modern world: the production of books and reading.

Whether you are more intrigued by the neat, poetic recipe of Jan Morris; the down-to-earth Pannacclety of James Herriot; or A. J. Cronin's Well Made Porridge, this is a book to dig into, to read in one go or consult for a particular recipe. This cook book is different from other cook books not only because these recipes come from some of the best known authors of our day, but also because they are not just recipes in the cooking sense. They are also recipes to stave off midnight hunger; to break up a working schedule; and to celebrate the end of a piece or book.

The NBL mounts Exhibitions in London; sends two or three hundred touring book exhibitions out across the country each year; answers 20,000 book queries annually; administers a plethora of prizes, including the Booker Prize, as well as organising the School Bookshop Association and the New Fiction Society; and it lobbies Government and Media in the cause of books and here it is benefiting from the sale of a book that should gladden any – stomach!

Read, eat and enjoy – – that is the motto of this book.

MARTYN GOFF

ACKNOWLEDGEMENTS

Very many thanks are due to all the writers who generously gave time and thought to help with this book and we are only sorry that it was not possible to include all the contributions. At the National Book League, Martyn Goff and Annie Cole-Hamilton, and at Transworld, Patrick Newman and Kathy Elgin gave enthusiasm and support. Shelley Woodyard followed up many of the permissions and Penny Phipps, Andrea Pomroy and Sally Muir gave great help with the typing.

Within the book we have been allowed to quote from many people's work: Eliza Acton's *Modern Cookery for Private Families* (Elek, 1966); Margery Allingham's *The Oaken Heart* by kind permission of Joyce Allingham; Anton's drawing from Desmond Briggs's *Entertaining Single-Handed* (Penguin, 1968); Edward Ardizzoni's illustration from *Long Ago When I Was Young* by E. Nesbit (Macdonald and Jane's, 1975); Elizabeth Ayrton's *Cookery of England* (Penguin); E. F. Benson's *Mapp and Lucia* (Heinemann, 1967) by courtesy of the Estate of E. F. Benson; Val Biro's drawing from Fanny Craddock's *The Sherlock Holmes Cookbook* (W. H. Allen, 1976); Quentin Blake's drawing from Patrick Campbell's *Rough Husbandry* (Hutchinson, 1965); Gyles Brandreth's recipe for Quyncys in Compost from Michèle Brown's *Food By Appointment* (Elm Tree, 1977); Brillat-Savarin's *Philosopher in the Kitchen* (Anne Drayton's translation, Penguin, 1970); Rachel Billington's *The Big Dipper* (Heinemann, 1970); Lucy Carne's *Simple Menus and Recipes for Camp, Home and Nursery* (Thacker, Spink & Co., Calcutta, 1919); *The Robert Carrier Cookbook* (Sphere, 1967); Frank Dickens' *More Bristow* (Beaverbrook Newspapers/Abelard Schuman, 1973); Nicholas Dimbleby's drawing from Josceline Dimbleby's *A Taste of Dreams* (Hodder and Stoughton, 1976); Tom Disch's poem from his collection *The Right Way to Figure Plumbing*; E.V. Knox's (Evoe of *Punch*) *Thestylis*, from a collection published by Allen & Unwin, (1976); Mrs Gaskell's *Cranford*; William Gerhardie's *The Polyglots* (Macdonald and Jane's, 1970); Giovanetti's Max cartoon from his *New Max Book* (Atheneum, New York, 1976); Edward Gorey's drawing from *The Unstrung Harp* within his anthology, *Amphigorey* (Putnam's, New York, 1975); Harry Graham's poem from his book *Deportmental Ditties* by courtesy of A. P. Watt; Graham Greene's *Ministry of Fear* (Heinemann, 1943, Penguin, 1972); Jane Grigson's *Charcuterie and French Pork Cookery* (Penguin, 1975); George and Weeden Grossmith's *Diary of a Nobody*; Dorothy Hartley's *Food in England* (Macdonald and Jane's, 1975); Barry Humphries' *Dame Edna's Coffee Table Book* (Harrap, 1976); Henry James' *A little Tour in France*; Paul Jennings' *Britain as She is Visit* (Hobbs/Michael Joseph, 1976); H. R. F. Keating's *Inspector Ghote Trusts the Heart* (Collins, 1972; Penguin, 1976); André Launay's *Caviar and After* (Macdonald, 1964); Robert Nye's *Falstaff* (Hamish Hamilton, 1976); Logan Pearsall Smith's *All Trivia* by courtesy of Constable Publishers; Richard Pennington's *Peterley Harvest* (by David Peterley) (Hutchinson, 1960); Pont's cartoons from *Pont: The Life and Work of the Great Punch Cartoonist* (Collins, 1969) by kind permission of Bernard Hollowood; Magnus Pyke's *Food and Society* (Murray, 1968); Heath Robinson's drawing by kind permission of Oliver Robinson; Helge Rubinstein and Sheila Bush's *Ices Galore* (Deutsch, 1977); Willie Rushton's *Superpig* (Macdonald and Jane's, 1976); George Bernard Shaw cartoon by kind permission of the Garnstone Press; Osbert Sitwell's *Great Morning* by courtesy of David Higham Associates; Sydney Smith's poem from Hesketh Pearson's *Thinking It Over* (Hamish Hamilton, 1938); Colin Spencer's *Gourmet Cooking for Vegetarians* (Deutsch, 1978); Mrs R. Temple-Wright's *Baker and Cook, a Domestic Manual for India* (Thacker, Spink & Co., Calcutta, 1912); Peter Tinniswood's *Except You're a Bird* (Hodder 1974); Ion Trewin's *Norfolk Cottage* (Michael Joseph, 1977); Alison Uttley's *Recipes From an Old Farmhouse* (Faber); Wyvern's *Sweet Dishes* (Himalaya Club Edition, Madras, 1881).

CONTENTS

CARVING.

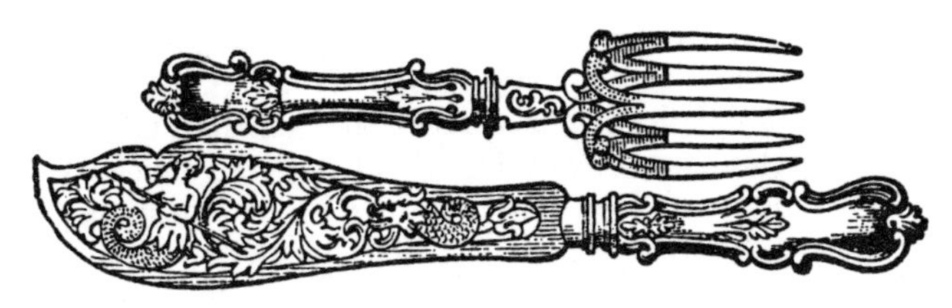

Fish Carvers.

Whether the passing fashion of the day exact it of her or not, a gentlewoman should always, for her own sake, be able to carve well and easily, the dishes which are placed before her, that she may be *competent* to do the honours of a table at any time with propriety and self-possession.* To gentlemen, and especially to those whc mix much in society, some knowledge of this art, and a certain degree of skill in the exercise of it, are indispensable, if they would avoid the chance of appearing often to great disadvantage themselves, and of causing dissatisfaction and annoyance to others; for the uncouth operations of bad carvers occasion almost as much discomfort to those who witness, as they do generally of awkwardness and embarrassment to those who exhibit them.

The precise mode of carving various dishes must of course depend on many contingencies. For a plain family-dinner, or where strict economy is an imperative consideration, it must sometimes, of necessity, differ from that which is laid down here. We have confined our instructions to the fashion usually adopted in the world.

Carving knives and forks are to be had of many forms and sizes, and adapted to different purposes: the former should always have a very keen edge, and the latter two prongs only.

* As this can only be accomplished by practice, young persons should be early accustomed to carve at home, where the failure of their first attempts will cause them much less embarrassment than they would in another sphere, and at a later period of life.

SIR HAROLD ACTON

FLORENTINE TORTINO OF ARTICHOKES

Born in Florence, I am naturally partial to all pasta, green lasagne, tagliatelle, spaghetti in divers ways, ravioli, cannelloni, etc, but, after careful forethought, this Florentine dish is most nourishing and variable.

Slice thinly and vertically 4 hearts of artichoke and allow them to thaw. Pat them dry in paper towels and sprinkle them with lemon juice. In a skillet or gratin dish heat 1 generous tablespoon of butter and 2 tablespoons of olive oil. Dredge the artichoke slices with flour and cook them slowly in the hot fat until they are a golden brown, which will take 4–5 minutes on each side. With a fork beat 4 eggs for about 30 seconds with salt and pepper and 2 tablespoons of milk or water. Pour the eggs over the artichokes and place the pan in a moderate oven at Regulo 4 (350°) for about 5 to 10 minutes, or until the eggs are set but not dry. Serve in the dish.

MARGERY ALLINGHAM

RECIPE FOR A PARTY

For some years then this annual jollification had constituted our only family holiday and was our one yearly reunion with all our hosts of old friends. We saved up for it like children, not only in money but in those precious odds-and-ends which one comes by in the country – a remarkable pot of jam, a vast marrow, new clothes, a picture one has painted or a dog kennel one has built, or even a lovely new joke. Sam coaxed his begonias to be at their best for it; Margaret and Chrissie saved their prize bottles of fruit for it; Mr Doe the butcher kept a special look-out for just the right baron of beef for the Feed, and down the road at Marshling the hams were picked out early for the same occasion. Every one of these little things was of extreme importance to us all, and I think rightly, for the genuine pleasures of life are elusive and seem to lie in the special occasions of commonplace amenities. They are the highlights, so to speak of the ordinarily good.

ELIZABETH AYRTON

ROAST CHEESE TO COME UP AFTER DINNER

This is Mrs Rundle's recipe of 1807 and very good it is too as a supper dish for four or a dozen savouries.

Blend together 3 oz sharp Cheshire cheese, 2 egg yolks, a teaspoon of made English mustard, 3 oz breadcrumbs and salt and pepper to taste. When the mixture is smooth, spread it on slices of toast (cut small if for savouries), cover with foil and bake for about 10 minutes at Regulo 6 (400°). Remove the foil and brown slightly.

Show your hands, Daisy.

BERYL BAINBRIDGE

INSTANT MINCE

I am a very bad cooker, as the children put it. It could stem from my father's habit of doing all the cooking at home – he wore his ARP uniform and made things like rubber egg and boiled tomatoes. However, I do have one recipe truly my own.

Take ½ lb of mince, 3 lb of potatoes, two sliced onions, a tin of tomatoes and a teaspoon of vinegar.

Throw the whole lot into a pan, though not the tin holding the tomatoes, and boil furiously for less than 15 minutes. Let the pan almost boil dry.

Cut one huge slice of fluffy white bread and spread thickly with butter. Spoon the instant mince on to the bread and cover with HP sauce, also raw onion rings.

Eat with a very strong up of tea.

SYBILLE BEDFORD

For the true lover of food, the dedicated cook, can there be any one dish singled out? Satisfaction, excellence have many forms, depend on the products of fields and sea, the weather, the place, the company. To me all food is a gift of the gods and has something of the miraculous; the egg no less than the truffle.

What I look for, in whatever country, in whose ever kitchen, are first-rate materials – in season, fresh, cooked according to their nature with simplicity, skill and taste, presented with large-hearted ease, eaten at leisure, in the evening, mind at peace, with friends.

In England, I like oysters and prawns; home-grown potatoes and vegetables; picked at dinner time and picked small (broadbeans the size of peas, and peas the size of pins) smoked fish, bacon and ham, game birds, spit-roasted; apples, cream, country cheeses. In America, roast sirloin on the bone (rib roast) savagely under-done, carved thick, never wafer shaved; clams, soft-shell crab, New England lobster, corn-on-the-cob, Virginia ham. In France, I like the serious scholarly attitude to food that survives at least in private houses. I like the modest hors d'oeuvres of a sliced tomato and a few rounds of saucisson, the soup of the evening, the chicken roast in butter without a trace of stuffing or sage (but then a chicken that's a chicken is almost extinct); I like the quick sautées and the slow-braised daubes, the little gratins and the vast regional dishes, potées and cassoulets and pots au feu and the aillouli and bourride of Provence, I like gigot roast saignant, garlic and sorrel, the occasional sauce honestly made without shortcuts and I like at least three-fifths of their three hundred cheeses.

I am interested in and much enjoy all oriental food; and most of all perhaps I feel at home with the Italian way of eating, their regard for texture and freshness, their respectful care of anything growing and green. I could live happily for a great many days on those young salad leaves, on hand-made pasta, grilled fish, Parmesan, mountain ham, peaches and grapes.

I detest minginess, cheating on quality, grey meat, soggy vegetables, anything over-cooked, over-herbed, over-sauced, over-elaborate. Nothing can go very far wrong at table as long as there is honest bread, butter, olive oil, a generous spirit, lively appetites and attention to what we are eating. There must be talk about food. I have not mentioned wine. Wine makes bad food tolerable, indifferent food unnoticeable, good food ... well no adjective: those who know do know, and those who don't would shrug. Good food then *and* good wine. And the better, the better.

E. F. BENSON

LOBSTER À LA RISEHOLME

Lucia's luncheon-party next day was to be of the nature of a banquet to celebrate the double event of her recovery and of the fact that Tilling, instead of mourning her approaching departure, was privileged to retain her, as Elizabeth had said, for ever and ever. The whole circle of her joyful friends would be there, and she meant to give them to eat of the famous dish of lobster *à la Riseholme.* It had already produced a great deal of wild surmise in the minds of the housewives at Tilling, for no one could conjecture how it was made, and Lucia had been deaf to all requests for the recipe: Elizabeth had asked her twice to give it her, but Lucia had merely changed the subject without attempt at transition: she had merely talked about something quite different. This secretiveness was considered unamiable, for the use of Tilling was to impart its culinary mysteries to friends, so that they might enjoy their favourite dishes at each other's houses, and lobster *à la Riseholme* had long been an agonising problem to Elizabeth. She had made an attempt at it herself, but the result was not encouraging. She had told Diva and the Padre that she felt sure she had 'guessed it', and, when bidden to come to lunch and partake of it, they had both anticipated a great treat. But Elizabeth had clearly guessed wrong, for lobster *à la Riseholme à la Mapp* had been found to consist of something resembling lumps of india-rubber (so tough that the teeth positively bounced away from them on contact) swimming in a dubious pink gruel, and both of them left a great deal on their plates, concealed as far as possible under their knives and forks, though their hostess continued manfully to chew, till her jaw-muscles gave out. Then Elizabeth had had recourse to underhand methods. Lucia had observed her more than once in the High Street, making herself suspiciously pleasant to her cook, and from the window of the garden-room just before her influenza, she had seen her at the back door of Mallards again in conversation with the lady of the kitchen. On this occasion, with an unerring conviction in her mind, she had sent for her cook and asked her what Miss Mapp wanted. It was even so: Elizabeth's ostensible inquiry was for an egg-whisk, which she had left by mistake at Mallards three months ago, but then she had unmasked her batteries, and, actually fingering a bright half-crown, had asked point-blank for the recipe of this lobster *à la Riseholme.* The cook had given her a polite but firm refusal, and Lucia was now more determined than ever that Elizabeth should never know the exquisite secret. She naturally felt that it was beneath her to take the slightest notice of this low and paltry attempt to obtain by naked bribery a piece of private knowledge, and she never let Elizabeth know that she was cognisant of it.

MICHAEL BENTINE

BENTINE'S CHICKEN WITH BRANDY PRUNES

6 chicken joints (thighs or breasts), 1 glass white wine, 1 dessertspoon wine vinegar, 12 prunes soaked in brandy, ¾ teacup finely chopped onion or shallot, 1 tablespoon chopped herbs (thyme, parsley, mint), a squeeze of lemon juice.

Place the chicken joints in a flat dish with the prunes tucked into spaces. Pour a marinade of the rest of the ingredients over and leave to soak. Cover the dish with foil and cook in a medium oven, Regulo 5 (375°) for ¾ hour. Remove the foil and cook for a further 15 minutes until browned. Serve with new or sauté potatoes and peas. (The dish can be prepared beforehand and cooked at the last moment.)

RACHEL BILLINGTON

THE LIGHT REFRESHMENT ROOM

'Aha!' The girl behind the counter in the Light Refreshment Room took his appointment card. 'Aha!' she repeated, studying it. Was there some mistake? But she bent down and drew out a mug and an inch high jug. Ian watched her movements closely and his mouth prickled.

'Bovril,' she read out, 'with tomato juice. And tonight yoghurt with wheat germ and honey.'

A tray passed over the counter; the cup of Bovril, steaming; the little jug of tomato juice.

Ian took it to his table. The Light Refreshment Room was like a glass conservatory built out into the garden. A goldfish bowl to be admired and envied from the outside. By those luckless wanderers still on lemon rinds wistfully sniffing a rose or turning a weak ankle on the gravel.

Ian sniffed. The heady smell of Bovril filled his nostrils. He poured the juice into the mug. He picked up the mug between his two hands. And then just for a moment he hesitated; he hesitated, mouth open, palate, quivering, stomach yearning. He must thrust it aside, knock the mug to the ground. Dash down the brew. But it was too late. Already, his tastebuds popped, his ears sang, his eyes watered. And the beefy mixture, rich mixture, glory of steaming heat, black liquid with scarlet trimmings, flowed, river of darkness, down his throat.

He had stepped backwards, downwards, inwards again. He put down the mug. Empty. His throat, he gradually became aware, was scalded and tingling. His head swam dizzily; there was a mist in front of his eyes. The room became dark.

'Drank it too quick, did you?' The black mists cleared before the sympathetic voice of a cleaning woman.

'I thought you'd fainted for a minute,' she continued as Ian stumbled to his feet. 'I don't hold with all this starvation bit,' she said with a conspiratorial look. I don't like to see people going hungry. I slip 'em something if they ask.' She followed Ian across the room with an insinuating closeness.

She reminded Ian of Rose. He didn't understand what she was saying, but she made him think of Rose and her Sauce Hollandaise which stood up in round turrets. Food, food. He went back to his room and down the long corridors, recalled the bar and the moments before the Bovril: the girl before the Bovril. What had she said? Yoghurt, wheat germ and honey. He remembered her words precisely.

His mind, which before had been as empty as his body was now writhing with words and images. Yoghurt, wheat germ, honey . . . But what time would it come? The hours in the hydro were generally early, almost hospital hours. It would probably be at six. In five hours. He had five hours to wait. Five long hours. He turned on the music, lay back on his bed and tried to turn off his mind.

But it wouldn't be turned off. The food he had eaten seemed to have set up an unutterable yearning which grew like home-sickness in his stomach.

He was waiting at the bar of the Light Refreshment Room when the girl arrived for the evening serving. He was early – although he had had to go back to his room for his card which in his haste he had forgotten. He had run along the corridor and his slippers had clapped against his heels so that he could still hear the noise in his head.

'Yoghurt, wheat germ and honey. Oh, you'll be getting fat on this!'

He watched the girl pile up the little round bowl.

SIR BASIL BLACKWELL

In the days of my youth and the Oxford heyday of Walter Pater, I overheard this conversation between two young men returning from a dignified dinner party:

'Conversation rather precious, wasn't it?'

'Yes, but I fancy I kept my end up.'

'Oh yes; but if you don't mind my mentioning it. Botticelli isn't a wine.'

'Isn't it?'

'My dear fellow, it's a cheese.'

VICTOR BONHAM-CARTER

SPICED CHICKEN FROM BRITISH COLUMBIA

I am one of those obedient people who will eat almost anything that is put before me; although I down tools when presented with tapioca or sago or brains. With the high price of red meat, chicken has become an all-too-common alternative and so it is essential to find interesting ways of cooking and presenting it. Here is one which I never get tired of and which is, I am told, not difficult to manage while still being unusual.

Cut up chicken and arrange in a flat dish. Sprinkle with salt and pepper, plus a dab of butter. Bake at Regulo 7 (425°) for about 15 minutes.

Mix in a saucepan: 1½ cups orange juice, ½ cup seedless raisins, ¼ cup chutney, ½ teaspoon cinnamon, ½ teaspoon curry powder. Simmer and add to chicken. Turn down oven to about 250 degrees for about one hour. Baste once or twice to keep chicken moist.

This is a very quick and delicious dish.

JOHN BOWEN

FISH PIE

I myself am an inexact and inspirational cook; some would say slapdash. My friends often arrive late and sometimes a dinner may have to be in two sessions to allow for some of the guests coming in after the theatre. Therefore, nothing that can be easily over-cooked. Many actors smoke, many drink spirits before a meal. Therefore strong, not delicate tastes. There is a fish pie, which I was first given by Tim Curry, but have since tried to make my own. Quantities will vary with the number of guests; the dish is a mixture of white fish and smoked fish with scallops and/or prawns or mussels, and some hard-boiled eggs.

Poach the white fish (cod, whiting, even coley) and smoked fish (haddock or cod; kippers are not a good idea) in white wine with pepper and a crushed clove or so of garlic, then poach the scallops for a shorter time. Remove, allow to cool, remove skin and any bones from the fish, and dispose in pieces at the bottom of a large casserole, together with one hard-boiled egg per person, halved.

Make a bechamel, using the cooking liquid instead of milk. Pour it over the fish. Open mussels by heating or shell prawns and dispose over the rest. Mash as many boiled potatoes as you think you'll need with a raw egg, butter, a little milk, and some grated Parmesan or Gruyère or even mature Cheddar. Make a thick crust of mashed potato over the other ingredients. Put in a hot oven about 20 minutes before you're going to start eating. Green Salad with it.

GYLES BRANDRETH

QUYNCYS OR PERIS IN COMPOST

Gazing at the typewriter in moments of desperation ('Mrs Beeton died at 28. I'm 29 and what have I done?'), hitting the typewriter in moments of black despair ('Keats died at 25. I'm pushing 30 and what have I done?'), I console myself with three thoughts:

alcohol at six, dinner at eight and to be immortal you've got to be dead.

I'm alive and I love food and drink. To me they're very real pleasures indeed (and I'm delighted to hear from my elders that they're also the pleasures that last) and because I find them such fun I'm able to use food as a carrot and drink as a carrot juice(?) in the never-ending struggle to get my work done. As writers go, I'm really quite disciplined: I set myself a target of so many words an hour and if I get behind schedule I don't give myself a tea or coffee break until I've caught up. On 'writing days' I have a light lunch and never drink until the day's work is done. With my first book, I had a celebratory meal at the end of every chapter. Now I've passed my fiftieth and have stopped counting, I don't celebrate until the whole book is done.

In the matter of food, as with everything else, I'm a very lucky individual. My wife is one of the world's great cooks. I eat like a king – quite literally, at times, since my wife has made a speciality of the favourite dishes of English monarchs since the Norman Conquest. You too can eat like a king if you have her book, *Food By Appointment*. Here's a recipe for a princely dessert that I love! I admit that 'Quyncys in Compost' isn't the most appetising of titles, but once tried it's never forgotten. And it's a dish that's stood the test of time: Henry VI (aged 8) had it at his Coronation banquet in 1422.

2½ oz whole stem ginger, 3 fl oz sherry, 22 fl oz red wine, 4 quinces or large, firm pears, 8 oz caster sugar, 8 oz stoned dates, 2 level teaspoons ground cinnamon, 1 level teaspoon ground ginger, pinch salt.

Cut the ginger into thin slices and leave to soak in the sherry in a covered jar for three days.

Peel the quinces or pears and slice into rounds about ¼ in thick. Remove core from each piece of fruit. Dissolve the sugar gently in the wine and heat until the syrup starts to thicken (about 15 minutes). Add the fruit to the wine and simmer gently until cooked but still firm (about 10 minutes). Add the dates, spices and salt. Continue heating without boiling until the flavours are thoroughly blended. Taste, and add more sugar if necessary. The wine should have a syrupy consistency and the fruit should be firm. Leave to cool.

Strain the ginger, reserving a tablespoon of the liquid. Stir this and the ginger into the wine syrup. Serve well chilled. (*Serves 6*)

NEVILLE BRAYBROOKE

'I'll have some lobster.' I was nervous. I was about to give my first lecture in an hour's time, and was dining with my Chairman at the Reform Club. When the waiter came to take our order, my Chairman said without so much as looking at either the menu or wine list: 'Two lobsters and a bottle of Vouvray.' A minute or so later the waiter returned to our table: 'No lobster on, Sir.' I looked again at the menu – this time with my spectacles on: I had misread 'homard' for 'home-made'. 'I'm very fond of home-made pie,' I spoke quickly so as to cover the general confusion: 'I'd just as soon have that.'

DESMOND BRIGGS

CHAMPAGNE PEACHES

Luxurious, yes, extravagant, yes, spectacular, ravishingly good and delightfully easy, also yes. Definitely a dinner-party pudding for when you want to impress but, if you work it out not quite as expensive as it sounds. Anyway, it suggests the grandest possible way of life for less than that normally costs and is absolutely no trouble. You could justify it to yourself by saying that you save on the wine, and another virtue is that it permits those who wish to smoke after the main course to do so while toying with thier peach, and those who don't smoke can still sip and toy – because, and this is its supreme virtue, it is a sipping – and – toying sweet. Serve after a rich main course, when everyone will want a pause.

You need one peach and ¼ bottle champagne per head. Chill each peach thoroughly, and, if you can the glasses also. Put one peach into a large wide wine-glass and, before serving the main course, prick each one all over with a fork.

Cover with chilled champagne and leave in the refrigerator if there is room. Serve.

Yes, but! The principle is that every guest takes their glass and toys with the peach, pricking it further with their fork. Of course, they sip. Of course, you top up with more champagne. After a few minutes of this delightful pastime (which also gives them something to do) the champagne gets more and more peachy and the peach more and more champagny. Also, the fuzz on the peach skin disappears and even an indifferent peach becomes something very luscious indeed. After all the toying and sipping, you can either mash your peach into the champagne or lift it out and eat it normally, skin and all. *Don't* serve either sugar or cream.

You can vary this with really good dessert plums or pears and if champagne is beyond the budget, peel and cube a fresh pineapple and put into the glasses, cover with dry wine and insist on the toying with the fork. In this case, they *may* need sugar, but still, no cream.

Serving Champagne Peaches.

BRILLAT-SAVARIN

THE DIFFICULTY OF MAKING GOOD CHOCOLATE

Very good chocolate is made in Spain; but we have stopped importing it from that country, because the Spanish makers are not all equally skilful, and the customer is forced to drink what he receives, whether it is good or bad.

Italian chocolate is not much to the French taste; generally speaking, the cacao is over-roasted, which makes the chocolate bitter and insufficiently nutritious, because part of the kernel has been burnt up.

Now that drinking chocolate has become universally popular in France, everyone has tried his hand at making it, but few have attained perfection, because the process is very far from being easy.

First of all, you must be able to tell good cacao from bad, and be determined to use only the best; for not even the finest quality cacao is entirely free from blemish, and misguided self-interest often overlooks damaged kernels, which should be thrown out to obtain the best results. The roasting of cacao is another delicate operation, and demands a certain tact not far removed from inspiration. There are some workers who are born with this skill and who never make mistakes.

A special talent is also needed for the proper regulation of the quantity of sugar which must go into the composition; no invariable rule can be laid down, for the amount must be varied according to the flavour of the kernels, and the degree of heat to which the cacao has been brought.

The grinding and mixing demands no less care, for it is on their absolute perfection that the digestibility of the chocolate partly depends.

Other considerations must govern the choice and quantity of the flavouring, which cannot be the same for chocolate intended to be taken as food, and for chocolate intended to be eaten as a sweet. It will also depend on whether or not vanilla is to be added to the mixture; so that, in order to make exquisite chocolate, a number of very subtle equations must be solved, which we profit by without even being aware of their existence.

For some time now, machines have been used for making chocolate; we do not believe that this method adds anything to its perfection, but it achieves a great saving of labour, and those who have adopted this method should be able to sell their chocolate cheaper. The contrary, however, seems to be the case; and this shows all too clearly that the real spirit of commerce is not yet naturalised in France, for in all fairness the advantage obtained by the use of machines should be equally profitable to the merchant and the consumer.

Being ourselves very fond of chocolate, we have run the gamut of nearly all the dealers, and we have now settled upon Monsieur Debauve, of No. 26 Rue des Saints-Pères; he is a purveyor of chocolate to the King, and we rejoice to see that the sun's rays have lighted on the worthiest of all. There is nothing surprising about that; Monsieur Debauve is a distinguished pharmacist, and brings to his chocolate-making all the learning he had acquired for use in a wider sphere.

BRIGID BROPHY

Bernard Shaw recorded that, having been 'a cannibal' for the first twenty-five years of his life, he became a vegetarian in 1880 or thereabouts, when the establishment of vegetarian restaurants in London made a change practicable for him.

By that token, all Londoners and most inhabitants of other parts of the British Isles should now become vegetarians. There is no shortage of vegetarian restaurants as such (though some of them are short of a licence, since some vegetarian puritans refuse to recognise alcohol as vegetable); and in almost any of the now ubiquitous Indian restaurants a vegetarian can remain free of blood guilt while sybaritically filling his belly with the spoils of the gorgeous East.

There has also been an outbreak, in British high streets, of health food shops. The health they purport to promote is human, and they are inclined to offer panaceas in the form of numinous seaweed or mystically gnarled roots from Tibet. But they also sell varied and tempting foods for people who deplore massacre, together with good-quality cosmetics not tested on the cat, rat and dog prisoners in our commerical concentration camps. At most of them you can get eggs laid by free hens, and many sell the take-away meals that save the energies of vegetarians households like mine, where everyone except me has a talent but none has the time for cooking.

There is in short not the least taint of austerity left to being vegetarian. It is the slaughterhouse that makes for monotony of diet, as it does for deadend imagination and covert connivance at violence. Slowly, slowly, we move towards England's greengrocerly and pleasant land.

JOHN BRUNNER

THE COMPLETE BRUNNER JAPANESE MEAL

Because writing is a very solitary occupation, I struggled for years with various musical instruments in search of a more direct contact with other people than the kind mediated through publishers and printers. I never became good enough even to perform at parties.

So when I realised I had the makings of a cook I was overjoyed. Here was precisely what I had been searching for – an art-form without tedious rewriting or editorial interference. And, even more to the point, instant verdicts from the audience!

Among the pleasanter discoveries which followed that initial revelation was that the Japanese have a peasant cuisine which tastes as good as their formal restaurant cuisine looks. Consequently I often pinch ideas from it. The following is not authentic . . . but I've been assured that it's delicious.

Eggdrop Soup

*

Simmered chicken *à la japonaise*
Turnips with vermouth (or saké)
Red and green pepper relish
Rice with mixed vegetables

*

Fresh fruit salad
Saké (or hot vermouth) – beer – gunpowder tea

For the soup
Take a left-over chicken carcase with a little meat still on it. Make a stock with rather less than ½ pint (3 decilitres) water per person – it will be supplemented; see below – plus about 1 teaspoon mushroom ketchup and 1 tablespoon soy sauce.

Just prior to serving remove carcase and add: 1 dozen peeled shrimps or prawns; 2 spring onions/scallions chopped, including the green; 2–3 button mushrooms sliced thin; 2–3 (5–10 cm) cucumber peeled and diced; ribs from 4 large lettuce leaves in ½ in (2 cm) lengths; 1 level tablespoon chopped parsley. (These ingredients are infinitely variable.)

Beat two large eggs with a splash of soy sauce. Stir the soup vigorously so that it swirls around the pan; pour in the eggs slowly enough for the movement to draw them into long strands. Serve at once – do not cook further.

No doubt the chicken (see next recipe) could equally well be parboiled in this stock; however, I'm not expert enough to keep dishes going simultaneously on every ring of the gas stove . . . so I tend to make soups in advance and only re-heat them when the guests arrive.

For the chicken
Joint one small bird, or use pieces. Parboil for about 30 seconds in water with a little soy sauce. Drain. Reserve the water.

In a shallow pan with a tight-fitting lid heat sufficient oil and brown the chicken pieces for 5–7 minutes. Pour off most of the oil. Add 3 tablespoons sugar; 2 tablespoons soy sauce; 3–4 tablespoons of the water used for blanching.

Use the remainder to make up the volume of the soup (above).

Simmer covered for about 10 minutes; remove lid and cook for about as long again but longer will do no harm. It comes out a filthy-looking blackish colour but it tastes fine.

If any is left over it is also quite edible cold.

For the turnips
Peel and dice (about 2–3 cm) 1 medium turnip per person. To 1 lb (approx. 500gm) turnips add 1 tablespoon sugar; 2 tablespoons cheap dry vermouth or saké; a little salt; water not quite to cover. Cook until tender in a pan with a tight lid. Meanwhile, steep a chopped and bruised clove of garlic with a pinch of salt in 1 tablespoon of soy sauce; 2 tablespoons water. Drain the turnips. Pour the dressing over. Keep warm under lid until ready to serve.

The last person who asked for seconds of this said in an injured tone, 'But I don't even *like* turnips!'

For the pepper relish
Core and seed 3–4 red and green peppers, assorted. Cut in strips about ½ in wide (1–2 cm). Boil in water with a splash of soy sauce until limp (15 minutes). Drain. Lay on dish and pour garlic or French dressing over and allow to cool.

For the rice
Cook about 2 tablespoons rice per person in slightly less than twice its volume of lightly salted water for about 20–25 minutes. Cook separately a small packet of frozen mixed vegetables. Drain. Turn off heat under rice. Stir in vegetables. Beat an egg and stir that in also. Replace lid. The heat of the rice will cook the egg on the way to the table.

Etcetera
I adapted the turnip and chicken recipes from *Japanese Country Cookbook* by Russ Rudzinski (Ryoichi Kokku) . . . where I also learned that 'Japanese do not normally eat sweets after a meal.'

That suits me fine. Fresh fruit, or a fruit salad, is recommended.

An admirable substitute for saké is to serve the rest of the vermouth used to flavour the turnips (for instance the Co-op's Ponti brand) hot and in very small cups. Also have on hand good beer, ideally Pilsner, and an aromatic tea such as gunpowder.

Whether or not to issue chopsticks is up to you.

ARTHUR CALDER-MARSHALL

IN PRAISE OF PERCEBES

In the bad old days before Franco banned beggars exhibiting the sores on their babies' bums, there was a café on the plaza at Vigo, where they served with each bottle of beer little platters of peanuts, anchovies, stuffed olives and, most delicious of all, 'Percebes'. Percebes look like bits of old electrical equipment; thick black insulation ending in what might be a fragment of discoloured porcelain, but is in fact the shell of the *Lepas anatifera* containing a complex of mouth, mandibles and long curled hairy feet, fascinating to the cirripediologist. The gourmet, however, will grasp the shell, remove the black insulation and take into his mouth the orange stalk in order to savour the incomparable flesh of the common goose-barnacle.

The only other place I have seen them is on the rocks of Santa Monica Canyon beach, where they proliferate in thousands, because Californians believe nothing is worth eating which is not sold in supermarkets.

JAMES CAMERON

I am the very worst person to write about food. I accept that eating is necessary, but the process gives me no pleasure. I think that the dilettante gastronome is the world's bore. I once spent a time in hospital when I was fed through a hole in my *arm*, if you please, and I loved it. No choice, no foolish menus, no meal times, just on and on like a browsing sheep. I can offer no serious contribution to the aesthetic of eating. What I live on mostly is bread, spread first with Marmite and peanut-butter, topped with chopped onion. I take this as a rule around 4 a.m., for I have the eating habits of an alley-cat, snatching things from the fridge and eating them in solitude.

However, if I am to nominate a celebrationary dish, for high days and holidays, it is as follows:

Grilled Fresh Herring: Recipe: take a fresh herring, preferably male, and grill it.

BRUCE CAMPBELL

Sometimes when I am in the mood,
I can eat any kind of food:
H. sapiens is omnivorous
And so, Good Lord, deliver us
From qualms on eating flesh or fish
When served in an attractive dish.

George Bernard Shaw eating letters.

PATRICK CAMPBELL

EARLY MORNING TEA TIME

Of all the times for refreshment in the home early morning tea, to the conservatively minded, is the one that must be run to inflexible rule.

To those to whom tea is served the slightest deviation from the norm works like sandpaper upon a nervous system already strained by the ascent from the soft valleys of sleep to the dizzy and jagged heights of consciousness.

Such persons have their 'own' cup, which is used for morning tea and for nothing else. The handle fits their flaccid morning finger, the circumference of the rim exactly matches the half-open, semi-waking mouth. Give them a larger or a smaller one and they actually get up, coming down as far as the kitchen, to ask what the hell is going on.

For those who make their own tea the pattern must be just as rigid. While they are making it the kitchen has to be devoid of human kind. If they are accustomed to having the tray set for them by somebody else, a missing teaspoon can lead to a clashing in the cutlery box that will – and is intended to – wake the whole household.

But however diverse may be the idiosyncracies of the two groups, they are passionately united upon one point of order. If morning tea is served, or made, at 8 o'clock that is the precise time at which it will occur, and until that precise moment no unusual disturbance of any kind must take place.

People waiting for tea in bed are prepared to tolerate, even to enjoy, the popping of gas and the chinking of teacups, knowing it is all for their own good. A sudden, inexplicable and almost inaudible conversation, however, with someone who may or may not be the milkman, infuriates them to the point of getting up and shouting for silence down the stairs.

In the same way, for those who make their own tea, a premature cry of greeting from above, or the running of a tap when the whole household should be asleep, is as shocking an intrusion upon their semi-consciousness as the firing of a gun.

Tea Time.

LUCY CARNE

HOT WEATHER LUNCH TEA

These are advisable in the hot weather in the plains, as one does not feel inclined to sit down to a meat meal during the hottest time of the day, so the 'lunch tea' at 3 p.m. is refreshing and gives one time to take a rest from 1 to 3 p.m., which is very necessary after a very early morning march, as one must get to the end of one's march by 8 a.m. Have tub, and breakfast about 10 a.m.

Lunch Tea No. 1

Tomato or cucumber salad
Toast or biscuits and cheese
Lettuce sandwiches
Cake. Tea with cream

Salad. Have the tomatoes or cucumbers put into a *ghará* of cold water till lunch time. Peel and slice up the tomatoes, etc., and dress with this sauce: One tablespoonful of sweetened vinegar, one pinch of finely-minced onion, one tablespoonful of salad oil, pepper and salt. To peel the tomatoes dip them in hot water for a minute or two; this will loosen the skin.

Cheese. When the cheese gets dry it is nice grated; in fact, I think it is more wholesome grated.

Lettuce Sandwiches. Take the tender leaves, place on thin bread and butter after dipping each piece in a dressing, sprinkle with grated cheese, place another piece of bread and butter on top and cut in shapes.

When there is a shortage of butter, jam sandwiches are quite good, but they must be made fresh.

Savoury Sandwiches. Mash up hard-boiled eggs with a good spoonful of anchovy essence and a lump of butter the size of a walnut, season with pepper (no salt), spread the mixture on brown or white bread and butter.

Salmon and sardines can be used in the same way, first bone and skin and mash them up with a bit of butter and add a few drops of vinegar and salt and pepper, then mix with the hard-boiled egg.

Cream for Tea. Take the cream off the fresh morning's milk just before tea, put it in a wire sieve and work it from side to side gently with a spoon, but do not rub it through. Use the strained cream for tea or coffee and the thick cream can be put away in a wide-mouth bottle for butter.

Butter. This everybody knows how to make in a bottle, but few know how to keep it in a solid state in the hot weather, so have to give up taking or making butter altogether. I have seen it served in a liquid state in a saucer! After the butter is made, wash it in filtered water with a little powdered Californian borax; salt, and put into an aluminium tin; close down firmly and place in a new *ghará* filled with cold water and sink it underneath your soda-water bottles. Place the *ghará* in the shade in the verandah where there is most wind. Two or three 'Blanco' tins do nicely for butter and fit the necks of most *gharás*.

J. L. CARR

SPICE LOAF

Well – and I'm telling you this only because you ask me – I'm a great believer in tradition so, each Christmas, my wife Sally bakes a couple of spice-loaves using my mother's recipe. She was Elizabeth Welbourn, an East Riding woman who lived at Corpse Landing not far from Winifred Holtby's home. (Tome Holtby was the county coroner.) And she had this recipe from Rachel Cole, *her* mother and I suppose she . . . well, I won't go on. So I eat it with emotion as well as Wensleydale cheese. As a matter of fact, when I was a little lad in the North Riding, I remember a poor girl called Alice coming round the houses, with a doll in a shoe-box, and singing at our back-door.

> 'Send forth the butler of this hoose,
> Put on his golden ring,
> And bring me oot some good spice-cake,
> That better I can sing.'

Poor Alice was the last of the true Wassailers. Commercial enterprise was a great preserver of tradition, whereas nowadays the deserving poor only have to fill in a form.

As a matter of fact Sally, who is a compulsive eater, met her first writer whilst eating spice-cake. In 1946, she was in Yorkshire for the first time, pursuing the tenancy of a cottage and this meant changing trains at Malton to go up to Goathland. There were two coaches of non-corridor compartments and she was the only passenger. Then a wild-looking man ran on to the platform and, rejecting all the empties, sat opposite to her. She already was eating her snap (as they call casual meals up there) and as she is shy, she began to look at a Penguin. He coughed and shuffled his feet and became very restless but when the pick-up came it was quite unusual. He said, 'Pardon me but are you enjoying your book?'

She replied, 'I haven't got into it: I just picked it up from *my husband*'s bookshelf. And this quietened him down till Levisham (which is just over the moors from Laurence Sterne's parsonage). Then he said, 'Well, you mustn't mind me asking, but you see I wrote it.'

In those days Penguins had a picture of the author on the back-cover so she took a quick glance and he was right – he *had* written *Three Fevers*. So she and Leo Walmsley shared what was left of her spice-cake (although he remained sitting in the opposite corner) and he told her his publisher had sent him to Fylingdales to finish a book.

Actually, he makes the second writer I definitely know has been paid by a publisher to go away to a nice quiet place. The other was John Ferguson who wrote Penguin detective stories and the play, *Campbell of Kilmhor*, and he had been sent down to Cerne Abbas. I was an utter stranger and, as we walked down the village street, he told me the plot of his next novel. Personally, I can't understand it: I have had five publishers and none of then has shown the faintest concern whether I lived or died.

If any southerner wants to know how to make a spice-loaf, they will need: 1½ lb of plain flour, ¾ lb sugar, ¼ lb butter, ¼ lb of lard, 1 lb currants, ½ lb sultanas, ¼ lb peel, ¼ lb ground almonds, 4 eggs, 1 teaspoon baking powder, 1 teaspoon mixed spice, ½ teaspoon bi-carb and 1 tablespoon syrup. You rub the fat into flour seived with baking powder then mix in the dry ingredients. Beat the eggs and with the syrup, add them to the mixture. Mix the soda with a little milk to make a stiffish mixture. Put into a greased and lined tin and bake at Regulo 4 (350°) for the first hour, and at Regulo 2 (300°) for the next 2 to 2½ hours. You eat it with butter and cheese, and never before Christmas Eve. And then only after you've eaten your frumerty.

ROBERT CARRIER

PASTA E FAGIOLI

½ lb dried kidney or haricot beans, 1 beef marrow bone (about 4 in long), 4 tablespoons tomato concentrate, 2 quarts cold water, 1 Spanish onion, 1 clove garlic, 3 tablespoons olive oil, 2 tablespoons chopped parsley, 1 tablespoon dried oregano, ½ lb broken macaroni, salt, fresh black pepper and cayenne popper.

Soak the dried beans overnight in cold water. Drain. Combine beans, marrow bone, tomato concentrate and water in a large saucepan. Bring to the boil; lower heat, cover and simmer for 2 hours.

Chop onion and garlic finely, and sauté in olive oil until transparent. Add finely chopped parsely, salt, pepper and cayenne pepper to taste and oregano and simmer, covered, for about 20 minutes. Add macaroni and continue cooking until tender. Serve sprinkled with Parmesan cheese. (*Serves 4.*)

BARBARA CARTLAND

CHICKEN WITH ORANGE SURPRISE

This is an absolutely delicious dish and delightful to look at. The first mention of oranges appears in the writing of the Arabs. They were introduced into the Western hemisphere by Chrisopher Columbus when he established a settlement on the island of Hispaniola in 1493. In England they were raised from seeds brought into the country by Sir Walter Raleigh. Oranges are full of Vitamin C which is essential to good health.

3 lb chicken
2 thin-skinned oranges
1 onion peeled and sliced
2 tablespoon golden syrup
1 level tablespoon cornflour
¼ pint orange juice
¼ pint cider
1 teaspoon ground ginger
fresh ground pepper
butter or sunflower oil
orange segments to garnish
½ teaspoon salt (sea)

Mix together ginger, salt and pepper and rub into the chicken. Roast at Regulo 4 (350°). Melt the butter and sauté the onion and finely shredded peel of half an orange until clear. Blend the cornflour with a little orange juice, add the remainder of orange juice and cider. Bring to the boil stirring. Blend in the golden syrup. Remove chicken from the oven and cut into pieces. Pour over hot sauce and garnish with orange segments.

JOHN STEWART COLLIS

RED CABBAGE WITH WINE

Clean and shred one head of red cabbage. Fry one chopped onion in 4 tablespoons of margarine. Add cabbage, 1 oz peeled and cored apples, 1 glass red wine, 1 tablespoon sugar, salt and pepper, simmer until tender. Then thicken with a little flour mixed with stock or water. Cooking time one hour. Delicious served with pork or boiled ham.

SHIRLEY CONRAN

ESAU'S POTTAGE

I like this because it tastes quite different when hot to when it's cold, so you have virtually prepared two dishes at one go. It's very cheap and easy – in fact a family favourite. When I get towards the end of a book I tend to *live* on it.

Boil 1 lb lentils according to the packet directions (which can be from ½ to 2 hours) until they are soft but not mushy; do not strain.

Add ½ lb sliced onion, 2 lb chopped tomatoes (preferably peeled if you have time – or you can use tinned tomatoes) and a dash of thyme and parsley. Boil for a further 10 minutes.

Add 3 oz butter and 1 oz grated cheese, then serve immediately. It's not a soup that keeps.

CATHERINE COOKSON

I gave up me piece of cake each day in order to melt me inches away; me liver pâté, taties and spotted Dick got the go-by pretty quick. Yet to go on living one must eat, and I was simply dropping on me feet; so I took to cheese washed down with wine, and everything was going fine; add an orange, apple, and some nuts, I knew me inches would experience cuts; but imagine my startled gasp when a hook of me skirt I tried to clasp. From thirty-one to thirty-three me waist had gone up on me. As for me hips, well, such roundies you never did see.

How comforting is cake and liver pâté and spotted Dick and things like that. Every man to his fancy, I say, cos I've got me inches either way.

LETTICE COOPER

HOME-MADE PÂTÉ

1 lb shin of beef, 1 cupful of fresh breadcrumbs, 1 onion, 2 cloves of garlic. As much red wine as you feel like sparing, up to half a bottle, grated rind of half an orange, and grated rind of half a lemon.

Remove any fat or gristle from beef, and stew very slowly in the red wine with water added to make enough liquid with onion, garlic, bay leaf, and any other herbs you like.

When the meat is soft, remove the bay leaf and squash the meat with a wooden spoon or mince it if you want it finer. Put it in a bowl and add breadcrumbs, all liquid from stew and rest of orange or lemon or both. Add a beaten egg and stir all together.

Line a fire-proof dish with strips of bacon. Press meat mixture well down into it. Cover with strips of bacon and a bay leaf or two and cook for about an hour at Regulo 3 (325°).

WILLIAM COOPER

When I come home from abroad, what is the meal I most pine for? It's true that so far as I recall it was reputed, when it first came in about forty years ago, to be Scandinavian. Now it seems terribly English to me. (Actually it requires, to be perfect, components you could only procure readily forty years ago.) For lunch you should assemble:

1 loaf of home-baked bread, preferably white
½ lb of farm Cheshire cheese
¼ lb farm butter
1 fresh lettuce
½ lb English tomatoes
1 pint of milk, slightly chilled

Everything should have the simplicity you only achieve by going to enormous lengths. For bread sliced plastic foam from the supermarket will not do; nor, for cheese, polythene-wrapped compressed sludge. The lettuce should on no account be dressed; you take off a leaf at a time and just dip it in a little pinch of salt.

That's all. You take a plate, a knife, a glass and go at it.

ALAN COREN

DINES OUT ON BEHALF OF ALL HIS READERS

My warm thanks to all of you who fired off recommendations from your own local patches, whither I shall be bearing the eager nosebag in the happy days ahead. For the time being, I thought I might trace my steps along the less-beaten tracks of that delightful *departement*, Gourmandy.

For while such parts of the province as Soho, Chelsea, Mayfair, Kensington, etc., are well-established as areas of lush provender, others are so unknown and hidden as to require guides not just to evaluate their offerings but also to walk in front of travellers with a red lantern and a megaphone, simply to lead them to these far-away places with strange-sounding names which they have never associated with good eating.

You may well, for example, decide to stroll down Greek Street or Beauchamp Place, with no particular restaurant in mind, and end up looking at one of a dozen worthwhile menus. But who in his right mind would stroll down Farringdon Road?

I should if I could be sure there was a table free at Bubb's which is as authentic a French restaurant as you'll stumble on in this quarter of the EEC: walk through its plain green door, and there you are in Arras or perhaps Clermont Ferrand, in one of those small, neat, austere but comfortable, basic but charming, totally professional restaurants that make life worth living in the less chic French towns. Dear God, if only we had them in Doncaster, say, or Kirkcudbright, or Goole, how much more delightful ex-metropolitan life would be!

Still *à cheval donné on ne regarde pas la bride*, so let us simply be thankful that we at least have one in London. Choose your meal over a glass of Kir, to my mind the only aperitif which will retire graciously from the tongue in deference to decent wine.

Just a half-mile south of Bubb's, as the gourmet flies, lies South Of The Border. Or, rather, nestles South Of The Border, tucked away as it is among the Waterloo warehouses of which it was once, before conversion from a bed-spring factory, a professional colleague.

Now, normally, you'd be fully entitled to shudder at the thought of something called South Of The Border, conjuring up as it does waiters in lurex ponchoes serving unauthentic *tacos* to the sound of castinets. But there is, thank heavens, nothing Mexican here; the name merely indicates, with typical South London defensiveness, the geography. Start with artichoke soup, if it's there, or Arbroath smokies, which certainly will be, since it's the one dish the customers will not allow the restaurant to withhold, with good cause.

MARGARET COSTA

TWO GRACES

On china blue my lobster red,
Precedes my cutlet brown,
Which with my salad green is sped
By yellow Chablis down.
Lord if good living be no sin,
But innocent delight,
O polarise these hues within
To one eupeptic white!

(Stephen Gaselee, Grace during a meal in Calais, Palm Sunday, 1938.)

With thankful hearts, O Lord, we ask that we
May never dine without remembering Thee;
And, grateful for our comfortable state
May leave no Lazarus hungry at the gate.

(Anon, Grace after meat.)

CHELO KEBAB

In the '50s, when I was Associate Editor of *Look Magazine*, I attended the trial of Premier Mossedegh. While there, I learned to eat the national Persian dish called *Chelo Kebab*, which I've never forgotten. It was, in fact quite impossible to find anything else served in restaurants then, as it is a tradition (*Chelo Kebab* to the Persians is like pasta to the Italians, honoured with the same devotion). I have kept the dish in my life since then, offering it successfully to friends whose food tastes are global. It can, by the way be made with chicken instead of lamb, using crisply boiled sections of the bird.

For each person: 1 cup cooked rice, 4 thin slices (gently salted) lamb, 1 cup yoghurt, 1 tablespoon finely diced raw onion.

At each place at table: 1 small raw onion, peeled but not sliced, 1 raw egg, top removed, in an egg cup, a little powdered saffron.

Two days before serving: Marinate *very* thin slices of lamb (cut in strips 2 in by 6 in, in yoghurt which has been mixed with finely chopped onions. Keep in ice box for two days before using. (For non-yoghurt lovers, marinate in lemon juice.)

At Dinner: Put a warm plate with a fat lump of butter in front of each guest, before passing round steaming hot rice. In the meantime, someone in the kitchen is broiling the lamb slices in a *very* hot oven, very briefly. If the lamb is tough, it should be scored with a knife before broiling.

Each guest spoons the rice *over* the butter, makes a little round dent in the rice, drops the raw egg into the dent, quickly mixes rice, egg and butter together, and shakes saffron over all. Then the lamb is served – presumably so tender that it can be cut with the edge of a fork. Those who like onions can put the raw onion on to the same plate and cut off pieces to add to the lamb and rice with each bite.

Footnote: Persians like to drink dugh with Chelo Debab, and the adventurous may wish to try it. It is made with yoghurt mixed with either still water, or the sparkling bottled mineral water.

FANNY CRADDOCK

MR SHERLOCK HOLMES' HOUSEKEEPER REVEALS THE SECRETS OF 'HER KEDGEREE'

½ lb cooked Patna rice, 4 hard-boiled eggs, 4 heaped dessertspoons freshly chopped parsley, salt and pepper, 1 lb either steamed, skinned and flaked salmon or smoked Finnan haddie, 5 oz good sweet butter.

Turn the cooked, strained rice into a roomy mixing bowl and add thereto the chosen fish, the parsley and a seasoning of pepper only for Finnan haddie, salt and pepper for the salmon. Shell the hard eggs, remove the whites from the yolks and chop up both quite separate and very fine. Season with salt and pepper. Melt the butter very slowly in a pan immersed in an outer pan of boiling water, so see that your kettle be singing upon the hob before embarking on this recipe. Work all together the contents of the bowl. Turn on to a heated dish. Then, with a fork held in each hand work up into a neat panel, fairly high and rising to a central ridge. Take up the hard, chopped egg yolks and use them to form a narrow border all around the base of the Kedgeree. Take up the whites and do likewise round the outside of the yolks.

It is then a pleasing fancy to have ready eighteen carefully shelled prawns with their heads left on. Before using these pour the melted butter slowly and evenly over and throughout the kedgeree. Finally arrange the prawns, heads erect down the 'spine' of the Kedgeree and send thus to the table, remembering to provide finger bowls of luke-warm water so that the fingers which come into contact with the prawns may be dipped therein and wiped dry upon a napkin.

A *Recommendation:* This recipe was warmly recommended by *Pipeline,* the quarterly journal for members of the Pipe Club of Great Britain whose reviewer acclaimed it as 'the best kedgeree recipe I've ever read'. He went on to say that 'pipe-smokers will certainly appreciate the many fireside cordials and beverages' and suggested that the book 'would make an ideal present for a pipeman's wife should he be feeling guilty about buying himself a new meerschaum for his collection'.

A. J. CRONIN

WELL MADE PORRIDGE

When I was young and poor, my favourite dish was caviar accompanied by a half bottle of Bollinger. But repetition destroys any pleasure, gastronomic or sexual, and now I have no favourite dish having eliminated all my 'favourites'! Now I like nothing better than a bowl of *well made* Scottish porridge, accompanied by a glass of good sweet milk, 'supped' in spoonfuls in turn. Delicious, good *and* nourishing and without after-effects.

Porridge to perfection comes about by stirring a cupful of pure, fresh milled oats into a saucepan containing four cupfuls of *cold* water. Add a teaspoon of salt and bring to the boil. Simmer stirring often for about 4 minutes, until creamy. Proper Scots eat this with a sprinkling of salt, but lesser mortals might prefer brown sugar and cream or milk.

ANTHONY CURTIS

Also Literary Editor of the *Financial Times*

MUSHROOMS SARAH

I find my mouth watering more at the thought of starters than main courses, however succulent. A particular favourite is a non-rich version of mushrooms *à la greque* devised by my wife and hence named after her. You make it as follows:

Skin and slice sufficient mushrooms to feed your numbers. Then steep them, stirring occasionally, for two to four hours in a marinade consisting of two thirds olive oil, one third fresh lemon juice, fresh ground salt, fresh ground black pepper and a dash of wine vinegar to taste. The mushrooms absorb most of the marinade and the mixture looks particularly attractive in a wooden bowl. Serve with hot garlic bread.

LIONEL DAVIDSON

THE BRETON FART

This great confection was made by one French novelist, Colette, and passed on to me by another, Tereska Torres. 3 eggs, a glass each of flour and milk, 4 heaped tablespoons of sugar, a pinch of salt. Put the flour in a bowl, make a hole in it and pour in the sugar, salt and eggs; then gradually add the milk and mix to a liquid batter. Pour this mess on a greased dish and leave for 45 minutes; then put it in the oven at Regulo 5 (350–400°) for an hour. Take out, sprinkle with sugar and tear apart and eat as soon as cold enough to handle. You never tire of the wonderful and delicate flavour. The name comes from the sounds it makes while cooking.

LEN DEIGHTON

COOKERY BOOKS

My first recipe book was the *Radiation Cookery Book*, published by a gas stove manufacturer. Using this, I amazed my parents by preparing quite complex meals at an early age. But I have to admit that this is a foolproof book. If anything goes wrong when you're using it, you need either new spectacles or a new stove. When talking to professional chefs I've often found that this same book was their starting point too.

Of course it is a long way from the magnificent *The Art of French Cooking*, probably the greatest work of its sort. Here over three thousand recipes have been collected together, recipes from Careme who cooked for Napoleon, from Urbain-Dubois 'master of the kitchens' of William I, the German Emperor, from Escoffier, for Ali-Bab, and so on. And the collator and translator have preserved, in so far as possible, the original text of the receipes, rather than make them conform in style.

For cooks who prefer one man, one book, there is *Modern Culinary Art* by Henri-Paul Pellaprat. It's another huge tome and I use it often. My only criticism being that the translator has entirely removed the original French menu name of the dishes, so that *Rognons de veau à la Grand-mère* has become Grandmother's Calf's Kidneys, and so on. Although Pellaprat has written many books, this one is usually called 'the Pellaprat' just as the previous book I mentioned is known in France as the 'Flammarion'.

These books are all-embracing. (In a flippant mood, I chose the Flammarion as my book for a desert island.) But they are not books one would normally see in the kitchen of a great French restaurant, where small reference books such as *Le Manuel du restaurateur* are enough to remind the skilled chef of things he's already learned. A typical entry under Rognons: *'Chateaubriand – Rognons grillés, sauce Château, pommes soufflées, cresson'*.

A thick, and rather grand version of this sort of book is *Haute Cuisine* by Jean Conil. It is in English and contains an immense amount of valuable information, as well as the listed dishes. Conil has a slightly different Rognons Chateaubriand: 'grilled, served with watercress, straw potatoes, cohered sauce'. As soon as one gets into translations there comes the problem of how much to translate. *Pommes paille* are 'straws' of thin deep-fried potato in the parlance of the chef. It takes a moments thought to understand that these are 'straw potatoes'.

Taking this sort of reference book one stage further, you have Escoffier's *A Guide to Modern Cookery*. No more lists, here the recipes are terse but complete. However, like so many compromises it is unsatisfactory; I'd rather go to the lists for inspiration, or to the Flammarion for education. But for real education in the science of cooking, one has to turn to the sort of book designed for use in catering schools. *Food and Cookery* is a typical textbook and an excellent one. But when that great gourmet and novelist Richard Condon (who also wrote *The Mexican Stove* a remarkably good cookery book) recommended *Understanding Cooking* I found it great fun. The book is arranged in such a way that a strip of paper reveals each answer as you read down pages of questions. Like a teaching machine (which indeed it is) it systematically informs and reinforces one set of facts after another, so that each question provides the answers too.

If that sounds too strenuous, there are plenty of books for browsing. The dottiest, and in a way my favourite, is *Real French Cooking* by a Paris journalist who writes under the name of Savarin. For a taste of the real Brillat-Savarin try *The Philosopher in the Kitchen*. The Americans are experts at writing about food (as against writing about cooking). A fine example of this expertise is Waverley Root's *The Food of Italy*, a 750-page treatise by a newspaper reporter dedicated to gastronomic research. H. M. K. Fisher is not so much a researcher as an essayist using the theme of food. *The Art of Eating* is a collection of the best of her writing, some of it going back to the nineteen-thirties but it remains fresh and witty and is the perfect antidote for a head that aches with recipes.

British cookery writers have excelled in writing about the history of food. Dorothy Hartley's *Food in England* is nothing less than a masterpiece however you measure it. Skill, charm, scholarship and all the tenacity of the researcher are evident on every page. If it is new to you, I envy you your first sight of it. And I found Drummond's *The Englishman's Food* quite 'unputdownable' as they say in publisher's adverts. And if it is English recipes you want, you'll do no better than the fine books of Florence White including *Good Things in England* and *Good English Food.*

My family like Italian food very much, so the books of that chef, writer and *restaurateur* (of George's in Rome) Vernon Jarratt are well thumbed. They range from the biographical *Spaghetti in My Hair* to *The Complete Book of Pasta.* Even the coffee table book, *Italian Regional Cooking* is regularly referred too. The only other large multi-colour cookery book that we actually read is *Masterpieces of French Cuisine* (a translation of *'La Cuisine aux Etoiles'*). It was published in English as a giant soft-back book, with photos and recipes from France's fine restaurants. Such books are usually a dismal bore but there had to be an exception sometime, and this is it.

I'm coming to the end of my space and you are perhaps wondering why I've not mentioned Elizabeth David, or Beck, Bertholle, Child or *Larousse Gastronomique* or Robert Carrier. Well none of those people need any plug from me. But perhaps Phillip Harben does. This man wrote some of the most sensible, practical and lucid cookery books we have in the English language. Many are in paperback, I urge you to read them all, particularly *The Way to Cook* or *Cooking*, a revised version.

And now two that I have to find space for, first the *Concise Encyclopedia of Gastronomy* put together by André Simon. There's a copy on the shelf of every cookery writer I know, and will answer nine out of ten questions put to them. In a quite different category is the slim and unpretentious *Home Baked*, enough to encourage anyone to make bread. 'Don't worry about draughts' they say and you don't and everything comes out fine.

After bread you'll be making croissants, Gugelhupf and Vienna Twists.

Finally let me tell you about the best cookery book of all. It's a loose-leaf volume which will provide endless ideas, realiable advice and precise cooking times. It conjures up memories of both delights and disaster, and provides hours of reading pleasure. There is even a version illustrated with drawings and photos. How do you get one – you write it yourself.

Bibliography (in order of appearance):

Radiation Cookery Book, Radiation Ltd.

The Art of French Cooking, E. Flammarion (compiler), Paul Hamlyn.

Modern Culinary Art, H. Pellaprat, Kramer, Paris.

Le Manuel du restaurateur (French language), H. Heyraud, Flammarion, Paris.

Haute Cuisine, Jean Conil, Faber and Faber.

A Guide to Modern Cookery, G. A. Escoffier, Heinemann.

Food and Cookery, R. J. Johnson, Dent.

The Mexican Stove, Condon and Bennett, Doubleday, NY.

Understanding Cooking, Ceserani, Lundberg and Kotschevar, Edward Arnold.

Real French Cooking, Savarin (pseudonym), Faber and Faber.

The Philosopher in the Kitchen, Jean-Anthelme Brillat-Savarin, Penguin.

The Food of Italy, Waverley Root, Atheneum, NY.

The Art of Eating, H. M. K. Fisher, World Publishers, NY.

Food in England, Dorothy Hartley, Macdonald and Jane's.

The Englishman's Food, J. C. Drummond, Cape.

Good Things in England, Florence White, Cape.

Good English Food, Florence White, Cape.

Spaghetti in my Hair, V. Jarratt, Frewin.

Eat Italian Once a Week, V. Jarratt, Frewin.

The Complete Book of Pasta, V. Jarratt, Michael Joseph.

Italian Regional Cooking, Ada Boni, Nelson.

Masterpieces of French Cuisine, F. Amunategui, Macdonald and Jane's.

Cooking, Phillip Harben, Penguin.

The Tools of Cookery, Phillip Harben, Hodder Paperback.

The Way I Cook, Phillip Harben, Frewin.

Phillip Harben's Cooking Encyclopedia, Phillip Harben, Odhams.

A Concise Encyclopedia of Gastronomy, André L. Simon (ed.), Collins.
Home Baked, G. and C. Scurfield, Faber and Faber.

KAY DICK

ON TEATIME

The meal I absolutely adore is tea, that much despised and rare feast, which brings out all my incipient indolence. Let us imagine summer, a green lawn, or a sandy beach will do – with exquisitely thin cucumber sandwiches straight out of *The Importance of Being Earnest*, followed by plates of equally thin bread and butter and Gentleman's Relish, topped by tiny iced cakes, pretty pastel shades, and fragrant Earl Grey with slices of lemon. And winter, with snow and roaring winds outside, a fire brightly burning one's toes, with delicious toasted crumpets soaked in butter which drips down one's cheeks, Ceylon tea this time, with rich fruity home-made cake, and indolence nothing but indolence in view: no time to think of the undelivered manuscript. Tomorrow will do for that lesser pleasure. And books around one: not those one should be reviewing or researching. Oh no! That would spoil the tea sensuality: let there be all the books one shouldn't be reading.

FRANK DICKENS

ROSE PETAL TART

You may feel this sounds too romantic to taste really good. If you have not yet discovered the subtle flavour of rose petals you have a treat in store. They have a definite flavour which is not too scented (some scented flavours can really taste too much like cosmetics). I first tasted delicious, delicate rose petal jam in Istanbul and my luggage on the return flight was overweight because I could not resist cramming in amongst my holiday clothes several pretty pots of jam with an old-fashioned picture of a crimson rose on the label. Since then I have realised it is easy to make one's own jam out of all those overblown roses which need snipping off throughout the summer. Then there are crystallised rose petals; pretty, unusual and subtle flavoured for decoration of cakes and puddings. The rose water you need for this tart can be bought at Greek, Cypriot and Turkish shops and also at chemists, and it is a nice addition to fruit salads. You can make the crystallised petals in advance and keep them in an airtight container until you need them. I think they are a delicious topping for this tart and everyone is amazed by them. The filling is rather like a very light, rose flavoured cheese cake.

For the petals: Beat an egg white until stiff. Put some caster sugar in a bowl. Dip each petal (1–2 red roses) in the egg white and then into the caster sugar, and lay on a non-greased baking sheet. Put in the lowest possible oven for about 1–1½ hours until quite dry and crisp. Ease each petal off carefully with a very thin knife, like a palette knife – some petals always crumble, as they are so thin and brittle. Keep in an airtight tin until ready to use.

For the pastry case: Roll out an 8 oz packet of puff pastry to about ⅛-in thick in a roughly circular shape. Grease a shallow flan dish (8–9 in). Line the dish with the pastry and neaten the edges by folding them over double. Cover the pastry with foil or greaseproof paper weighted down by dried beans or rice and bake blind in a pre-heated oven at regulo 6 (400°) for 15 minutes. Take off the foil and beans and leave to cool.

For the filling: In a mixing-bowl whip up ½ pint double cream until it is thick. Add an egg yolk, 2 tablespoons of caster sugar and a family-size carton of plain yoghurt and whisk thoroughly together. Gradually add 2 or 3 tablespoons of rose water and a few drops of rose essence to taste. Pour the mixture into the pastry case and bake in the centre of a pre-heated oven at Regulo 3 (325°) for 20 minutes. Cool in a fridge. Take out an hour or so before eating. Sprinkle the crystallised rose petals all over the top at the last moment.

TOM DISCH

INVITATION TO THE DINNER

All right, everybody, let's sit down
To dinner. Mike, you may pass
The potatoes. Hilary is there any
Gloucestershire sauce? Thank you. John,
That's your place, and this is mine.
I'm so hungry and everything looks so good!
Art has an important part in all our lives,
But it is never as important as dinner.
That is why I have made this poem a dinner
And invited you to it.

ROBERT DOUGALL

CHILLI CON CARNE

My wife Nan and I came across this dish on a trip over the Pacific in an American freighter three years ago.

It was our first experience of American menus. We found that they use three words where we use one. 'Steak' becomes 'Grilled western prime rib steak'. 'Mashed banana squash' turned out to be a vegetable called squash prepared like a mashed banana. Billy the huge, benign Negro steward from California always referred to melon ironically as 'Georgia ham' because in the bad old days that was about all the slaves there got to eat.

2 lb stewing steak, 3 tablespoons oil, one large onion, one clove garlic, salt, 1–2 level teaspoons chilli powder, 1 level teaspoon dried oregano, 2 level tablespoons plain flour, ½ pint beef stock (made with stock cube), 1 level tablespoon tomato purée, a 14 oz can tomatoes, a 15 oz can red kidney beans.

Trim meat and cut into smallish pieces. Heat oil in large saucepan and fry meat quickly to brown. Remove with draining spoon and set aside. Peel and chop onion. Peel and crush garlic to a smooth paste with a little salt. Fry onion and crushed garlic together until soft and transparent. Stir in the chilli powder, oregano and flour and cook, stirring for 2 to 3 minutes. Gradually stir in the stock, then the tomato purée and tomatoes. Return meat to pan, bring to the boil, cover and simmer gently for 2–2½ hours. Twenty minutes before the end of the cooking time add the drained kidney beans.

Serve piping hot on a bed of fluffy boiled rice. (*Serves 5 or 6.*)

PETER DRISCOLL

BAKED LAMB WITH HARICOT BEANS

When we were newly married my wife and I went to live near a small village in Corfu, the island with so many literary – particularly English literary – associations. Armed with only two gas rings, the produce of the local market and a copy of Elizabeth David's *Mediterranean Food*, Angela set about turning herself into an accomplished cook. In Corfu in those days frozed food was unheard of, tinned and packeted things were few and expensive. We shopped as the Greeks did – every day, for what was fresh and cheap – and ate accordingly to the rhythms of the seasons, including those seasons when such staples as onions, garlic, and even potatoes simply disappeared from the market.

Spring would bring young lamb, early potatoes, peas and beans, and cherries; in summer there were great quantities of mackerel and shellfish, squid and rubbery octopus which had to be beaten against a wall to soften it, peppers, aubergines, tomatoes, cos lettuce, courgettes with the bees still busy in their flowers (the flowers to be stripped off and fried as a separate vegetable), fish and melons. Autumn brought woodcock and snipe, the first pressing of new olive oil and wine, and in winter we kept warm on bean stews, fish soups and casseroles accompanied by the most gigantic cabbages and leeks I have ever seen. All this left us with a taste, sustained to this day, for food which is not specifically Greek, but Mediterranean in character. The cuisine is neither *haute* on the one hand nor limited on the other; it is based simply on the ancient produce of the region, olives and olive oil, fresh herbs, aromatics and wine.

This is one of Angela's original recipes based on traditional Mediterranean ingredients and particularly comforting for a British winter.

Soak 8 oz of haricot beans overnight and parboil them the next day. Slice some onions coarsely and lay them in a roasting pan. Scatter the drained beans on top of the onions. Salt and pepper the lot and pop a few bay leaves over the mixture. Salt and pepper 3–4 lb leg of lamb and rub all over with thyme. With the point of a sharp knife make small pockets in the joint, insert slivers of garlic. Lay the lamb on the bed of onions and beans. Open a 14-oz tin of tomatoes, halve the tomatoes and pour them and their liquid around the joint. Add a little olive oil in a trickle around the roast, and the quartered potatoes bedded into the tomatoes. Now add a couple of cupfuls of chicken stock into which you have mixed a dessertspoon of tomato paste. Put the whole dish into a pre-heated oven Regulo 5 (375°) and roast until tender – the lamb should still be pink inside. Baste the joint and potatoes frequently, and if they get dry add more stock – the beans absorb a lot of oil and juices.

Cut the lamb into thickish slices for serving, and see that there is a good helping of the bean and tomato sauce for each person. The potatoes should be soft and full of flavour. This is a complete meal in itself, needing nothing to accompany it but a squeeze of lemon juice over each portion, some red wine and perhaps crisp winter salad of chicory, onion rings, and sliced green peppers.

MAUREEN DUFFY

The greatest problem for an East Ender becoming a vegetarian, and brought up on a main meal of tea, is how to do without fish and shellfish, that flavour of sea-essence. You can have a very deathlike vegetarian banger but they haven't yet got round to a proper use of seaweed except in the traditional laver bread. That leaves us with real caviar; not the roe of gutted lumpfish but the real expensive thing laid like turtles' or any other eggs. Don't mess around with toast or lemon juice, just eat it very slowly and savouringly. It tastes like winkles. Once, in the days when I thought hunting manly, I caught and boiled my own winkles. They didn't want to die, poor stupid molluscs, and they didn't taste right. In fact I could hardly face them. They had clung to the rocks and then drawn their doors right shut against me and the omnipotence of boiling water. Caviar's so much better (though if anyone knows any horror stories about how it's done on the shores of the Caspian I'd rather they told me). There are still quails' eggs and they taste like crab meat. When I was a child I used to hunt crabs and bring them home in a bucket. They got out and wandered round the house looking for a way to the sea. Quails' eggs are rich, gamey, greasy, and best eaten with a little celery between each couple to cleanse the palate, much as my auntie always has bread and jam after kippers: 'to take the taste away'. You can buy them in tins already boiled and shelled. They keep a couple of days in the fridge when opened and therefore end up curiously economical. Quails' eggs and caviar, that's for Christmas.

DAPHNE DU MAURIER

CORNISH SLOE GIN

Gather sloes, when ripe, during the month of September here in Cornwall. Prick each sloe with a silver fork, and place them into a clean, empty, wine bottle, filling the bottle only a quarter full with the sloes. Then add two ounces of lump sugar, and two ounces of crushed candy sugar. Top up the bottle with Plymouth Gin until it is full. Cork and seal. Shake the bottle or bottles twice a day or more for three weeks. Then put away for six to twelve months, when it will be ready to drink.

This recipe was given me over forty years ago by Sir Arthur Quiller-Couch, who, with his family, regularly made sloe gin and laid it down at his home 'The Haven', in Fowey.

JANET DUNBAR

When I was a new bride – well, newish – we once entertained a gentleman, whom I shall call Mr D, to dinner. We had met him in the Cevennes, conducting a small party on their way to visit the ancient lady who had been, when young, Robert Louis Stevenson's landlady for one night during his travels with the donkey. When the melon season comes round and I have one, I still think of Mr D and wonder if his trousers ever recovered.

At that early stage of housekeeping you have the urge to try out classy-sounding recipes from magazines on a guest, and I tried out Filled Melon. You cut off a *tranche* from the pointed end, peel and cube it, remove the seeds from the main body, sit it on the blunt end, fill it with the cubes, and top off with a very light cream mixture that isn't heavily flavoured. Powder with caster sugar and cinnamon. To serve, cut slices vertically.

Well, I did all that and it looked good, a little symphony in yellow and brown. After the first course (I've forgotten what) I brought on the melon and picked up a knife. Mr D was giving my husband a mass of misinformation about Robert Louis. (I was brought up on R.L.S. and I was also brought up not to contradict my elders.) I cut down vertically. The melon slid off the plate on to Mr D's inadequately napkinned knees. Without the slightest hesitation he picked it up, replaced it on the serving dish and went on with what he was saying. I held down the melon with my left hand and cut vertical slices with the other. The conversation flowed on. Nice Mr D.

PS: Don't trust the blunt end *ever*. Cut a piece off and see that it's flat.

JANICE ELLIOTT

THAT CHICKEN THING

Since my idea of entertaining is absolutely not to fry my eyebrows over a hot stove while everyone else is honking in the next room, I fall back often on a chicken dish which may be ordinary, but can be prepared well ahead and never fails to be delicious. I can whip it up in ten minutes at sea. If it has a name, I don't know it. Chicken fricassée? *Poulet à la crème?* The family call it 'That Chicken Thing'.

Cooked chicken from a bird of about 6 lb, ¼ pint milk, ½ pint of chicken stock, 1 chicken stock cube, 1 glass white wine, 3 tablespoons cream, 2 oz plain flour, 2 oz butter, bouquet garni, ¼ lb sliced mushrooms or small tin of mushrooms, small packet of frozen mixed vegetables or small tin carrots or cooked carrots, lemon, seasoning of pepper, salt, celery salt, parsley dried or fresh to garnish.

Simmer chicken, nearly covered with water, in oven or on hob for 1½ hours, with bouquet garni. Save stock. Remove chickens from bones and leave either diced or in small portions. Make roux with butter and flour. Crumble in chicken stock cube and stir in milk and stock (both hot for a smooth sauce). Allow sauce to thicken. Add vegetables, then wine, seasoning and cream, stirring all the time. If vegetables are not pre-cooked, simmer for a further 20 minutes. Add chicken and generous squeeze of lemon. Garnish with chopped or dried parsley. Serve with rice, or better still, new potatoes.

This can be served hot or cold, or re-heated in a low oven. For a quick family dish, cold roast chicken left-overs may be used. Wine and cream can be omitted. This mixture also makes a good filling for pancakes (for convenience, the pancakes too may be cooked several hours ahead, then brushed with melted butter and re-heated in a buttered dish at Regulo 4 (350°).)

CHRISTOPHER EVANS

A FAVOURITE MEAL

Just as drab, unaesthetic surroundings can take the edge off even the most superb cooking, so a really congenial environment can turn the simplest of meals into a gastronomic delight. In my case the ideal environment happens to be somewhere with a bright hot sun, a blue warm sea, and a small, choice collection of attractive, nicely tanned companions. The meal framed by this environment is served in a beachside restaurant in a town in the Florida keys, and it is predominantly Mexican. To start there is a large crispy American salad with creamy Thousand Island dressing, and a bowl of blistering chilli (made with pinto beans and not too much tomato). This is followed by *tacos* (a kind of Mexican salad sandwich made out of cornmeal) and beef and chicken *enchiladas* – long soft pancakes in a rich cheese sauce. For dessert there is Key lime pie, or banana cream pie if they're out of the former, or both. Before, during and sometime after the meal there are bottles and bottles of ice-cold Mexican beer (Carta Blanca preferred) dispensed into frosted glasses. Bliss, just bliss for less than five dollars, beer excluded.

EVOE

THESTYLIS

We had a cook, but she has gone away,
She was too good, too beautiful to stay—
Beautiful in her art, I mean to say.
    There is no book
That can expound the sorrow of the thing
When a light hand with pastry taketh wing;
We can but sit and weep, remembering
    How she could cook.

It was a dreary and a winter morn
What times the taxicabman wound his horn,
And Thestylis, her trunk of tin upborne
    With a great push
On to the taxi, bade us both adieu:
Tomorrow to fresh woods and pastures new—
The actual place was in some avenue
    Near Shepherd's Bush.

Ay, Thestylis is gone, who had no peer
(Young Thestylis) in making thick or clear,
Or doing simply anything, my dear;

Why, she could scrub!
Ah, false and fickle as the white sea foam,
Why did her wayward footsteps choose to roam
Just when one got as good a joint at home
As at the club?

There was no sound of trouble when she went,
No observations on the way she spent
Her outings, and her work was excellent;
She did not leave
Through having words with Mary over spoons,
She got her ordinary afternoons,
She did not come to crave for extra boons
Like Genevieve.

She was not bribed away with alien gold;
We would have had the grand piano sold
To keep her. Then what ailed the girl? The old,
Old fatuous whim.
She had a friend. I count it a disgrace
That love should trench on Art in any case.
She had a friend. She took another place
To be near him.

Him at the dancing palace, Hammersmith,
It was her custom to go dancing with
(O vanished steaks! O mutton now a myth!)
And so she left.
Blunt is today the ineffectual steel
Because of that young man, and poor the meal;
The concave, soufflé tells the woe we feel;
We are bereft.

O happy basement where her feet are set,
Wherein she turns today the omelette;
Shall she remember or can we forget
Our too brief bliss?
The fricassées, the savouries, the stews,
The various cheer from which she bade us choose?
These mutton cutlets are like ancient shoes,
Ah, Thestylis!

But happier he and favourite of chance,
That youth who now attends her at the dance
And sees on Thestylis's countenance
        A lover's look:
He has no other thing for which to pray,
And, when he bids her name the happy day,
His lot it shall be roses and all may,
        For she *can* cook.

J. G. FARRELL

OMELETTE SOUFFLÉ V.S. NAIPAUL

Any sensible person early in life learns how to prepare a number of appetising dishes and cooks them so often that he can produce them almost automatically. One of the most satisfactory over the years from my cuisine (eggs being very often the only thing left in the refrigerator) has been the omelette soufflé. This particular one, based on the familiar 'Arnold Bennett' is made with gurnet instead of smoked haddock and was created in my kitchens in honour of the great West Indian writer and his wife. Gurnet is a gloomy and alarming-looking fish, but cheap and delicious, and with the firm flesh that is ideal for this sort of dish. However, if you cannot find (or be bothered to cook) a gurnet, a tin of red (not pink) salmon makes a good instant substitute and saves you a deal of palaver. The measures are approximate and can be adjusted to personal taste.

Pre-heat oven to Regulo 3 (325°).

Take a small gurnet from which you will be able to get, when cooked about 8 oz of flesh. Brush with oil and place in foil with a few spoonfuls of white wine or vermouth, pinching the ends over to seal it so that it will steam in wine and own juice. Place in oven and inspect after about 40 minutes prodding with a knife: when cooked the flesh will lose its glassy appearance and come off the bone, so debone it.

Place 6 tablespoons of cream in a saucepan and melt 4 oz of grated Cheddar into cream and remove from heat. Add the fish and a spoonful or two of its juice (or salmon plus juice from its can) to the cheese and cream mixture, then add yokes of 6 eggs and blend all together: the resultant mixture should be thick and creamy but not too runny: add a little more fish juice or cream if you need to make it more liquid. Add pepper, and one teaspoon of chopped shallots or chives if available.

Beat egg whites and a pinch of salt with a balloon whisk if you have one (it is worth getting one if not; it makes a real difference to the texture) into 'soft' peaks. Fold a quarter of this foam into the fish mixture, then fold fish mixture into rest of the egg whites.

Empty contents into heated and buttered frying-pan. Sprinkle top of omelette with grated cheese. After a minute remove from heat and place under grill until the omelette has puffed and browned on top.

The omelette should still be *partly liquid* inside. It is better to under-cook than over-cook. Over-cooked it will taste leathery and disappointing. Serve immediately with brown bread and butter and chilled white Burgundy.

DANIEL FARSON

A DOG'S DINNER

Once I had a driver. The reason for this indulgence was simple. I had passed my test but distrusted cars so much that I refused to drive them. Consequently, my late night arrests for being drunk and disorderly as I tried vainly to hail a taxi home began to vex my employers. So I advertised locally for a chauffeur. At that time I lived at Limehouse in a romantic cluster of derelict houses on the waterfront. Unfortunately they have become fashionable since then, owned by painters in smocks, trendy editors, successful paperback publishers, a 'TV Personality' personified, and even a Foreign Secretary. But it was peaceful in those early days and justified the arduous journey home, provided I could find someone to drive me. This was how I acquired Arthur and a large blue car. Arthur was large too, as strong as an oak door with shoulders as wide, always in a smart blue suit, white shirt, and black tie – even in the country. Strangers assumed he was some sort of bodyguard but he was the gentlest of men soon to be dominated by my whippet called Pencil whose melting eyes melted his heart accordingly. His other passion was a girl called Phyllis whom he suspected, with no justification whatever, of perpetual adultery. If he phoned her in the afternoon and the number was engaged, he became deeply disturbed and convinced that he could hear her talking to the 'other man' though I assured him this was technically impossible.

When I moved to North Devon his worries over Phyllis increased and he would have given me notice if it had not been for his devotion to Pencil and my other dogs. Finally, he did leave to marry her – but my love of food was also partly responsible. Arthur's only blemish, if it can be called that, was a detestation of food, as something to eat and even more as a topic of conversation.

He disliked his meals as much as Tony Benn who chose the buffet at Temple Meads Station when I asked him where he would like to have lunch in Bristol.

Like many Englishmen in fact, Arthur considered the subject unmentionable. He suffered most when I had guests to stay, particularly when Robert Carrier arrived for a long weekend with another friend of mine, Sandy Fawkes, who has achieved notoriety since as the near-victim of an American rapist and mass-murderer. Every morning we sipped wine after breakfast and chatted incessantly as we chopped and simmered. Every afternoon we went for a drive and discussed the meals we had just prepared. Arthur became more taciturn with our every mouthful.

When you have a famous cook to stay it is better to let him do the cooking rather than impress with any fancy speciality of your own, so the climax to the holiday was one of Robert's 'great dishes of the world', a *Boeuf à la Bourguigonne*, which he organised with his usual professionalism giving specific instructions to the startled village butcher on how to cut the top rump and the salt pork (no calf's foot was available); choosing the appropriate Burgundy; selecting the complementary vegetables. It was a star production.

As our contribution to the banquet, I was in charge of a simply baked salmon trout, with which it is impossible to go wrong, and Sandy conceived a light sweet for the final course. But the *Boeuf à la Bourguignonne* was the *pièce de résistance* and our anticipation must have seemed obscene to Arthur who heard us discussing it interminably as he drove us across the countryside in our search for delicatessens, greengrocers, calf's feet, and pubs. As we slobbered over food as if it was sex, I could see his mouth reflected in the driving mirror, tightening grimly.

On the great day, the earthenware casserole was placed reverently in the oven to simmer gently while we went for our drive and the dogs were locked up yet again. Robert Carrier started to laugh as he read an account in the paper of a disastrous dinner party given by a hostess who tried to impress her husband's boss with a tinned-salmon mousse but nearly killed him instead.

Suffering from instant food poisoning, the guests had staggered 'flailing' into the Chelsea Street where they collapsed until the screaming ambulances revived them. This set us off on a series of culinary calamities, such as the dinner given by Frank Lloyd Wright, if I remember correctly, whose butler stood behind the door with an axe and cleft the guests to death as they entered. The three of us sobbed with foolish laughter while the wretched Arthur who shared neither our sense of black humour, nor our fascination in food, nor our long friendship, stared stormily ahead and thought of the dogs imprisoned at home.

When we returned with our taste buds watering, I was sent to the garden for some herbs while Robert changed and went down to the kitchen to concentrate on the final stages of the masterpiece. A moment or two later I saw him coming up the drive: he looked puzzled. 'That's odd,' he said, 'it's disappeared.' When he explained that he was referring to the casserole, I must have looked bewildered too. 'It couldn't have been stolen, could it?' I asked fatuously, thinking in terms of a food spy – a possible lightning strike by Elizabeth David when we were out.

'How mysterious,' said Sandy when we broke the news. But it wasn't really. The answer became plain as several happy dogs returned from their food tray licking their chops with satisfaction. Arthur followed them and had the grace to look sheepish. 'Gave it to the dogs, didn't I?' he said. 'It *looked* like dog's food, know what I mean?' This was his excuse to which there was no answer, so we opened some tins for the main course instead while he took the dogs for a walk on the dunes, humming a merry tune.

I hope I have never been quite such a food snob since.

CONSTANTINE FITZGIBBON

POTATO CAKES

In the proper circumstances and the correct place – in this case some god-forsaken farmhouse in the West of Ireland, after a hard day of being misguided away from the 'antiquities', with rain beginning to fall outside but a lovely turf fire within what could be nicer than a high tea of 'rashers and hen-eggs and potato cakes', washed down with plenty of strong, Indian tea.

For the potato cakes you'll need 1 lb boiled potatoes. Mash them while they are still hot with a lot of butter and some salt and pepper, then add flour and beat that in until you have a dryish mixture that will roll out into a thick sort of pastry. Cut it into rounds and fry the rounds, preferably in bacon fat.

MARGARET FORSTER

ONION CREAM TART

I am not normally a nibbler but it mortifies me to admit that I only have to sit down at my desk to start thinking about snacks. I start work at 9.15 as the youngest leaves for school and I take into my office a tray with my breakfast on it and I sit and eat while I settle myself to work. Nothing exotic – a bowl of home-made muesli, cup of black coffee, and a thick slice of wholemeal toast with butter and Marmite. I regret eating it the minute I've finished. After an hour, I get up for a prowl around and take back an orange, after another hour it is an apple. I get very sulky and discontented towards the end of the morning if I know there isn't something nice to eat afterwards. I always felt ashamed that creative activity should inspire me to nothing but gluttony but now I've come to accept it as harmless compared to what it brings out in others.

My husband, Hunter Davies, drives me crazy when he is working at home with his desire for 'something delicious in the oven'. His tastes are more substantial than mine and run to hefty stews and thick soups and substantial puddings. Since he can't cook anything this leads to a lot of clashes. I lie – he *can* cook one solitary dish which is a quite nauseating thing called Hunter's Special. It consists of a slice of toast with cheese and ham on top surmounted by a poached egg. The entire kitchen is in a state of chaos while he makes it and the whole family discourage him as much as possible. One dish we both love which keeps me happy and him from furtively haunting the local delicatessens for rich pâté and chocolate cake is Onion Cream Tart.

Line a 7-in flan case with 6 oz shortcrust pastry.

Slice 1½ lb onions finely and put them into heated 1 oz butter and 2 tablespoons oil in a saucepan. Cook them very slowly with the lid on until they are soft and golden. Add a crushed clove of garlic and cook another ½ hour – the whole process takes about 1½ hours.

Remove onions from heat and add 1 egg plus 1 egg yolk, beaten with 4 teaspoons double cream and salt and pepper. Mix and pour into flan case.

Arrange 12 anchovy fillets in a criss-cross pattern on top and fill in with stoned green olives. Cook in centre of hot oven at Regulo 6 (400°) for 30 minutes.

Allow to cool slightly before eating – best warm.

CHRISTINA FOYLE

LEMON MOUSSE

This recipe is rather practising what I preach since experience has taught me that when arranging large, elegant functions one should be very careful to serve attractive food that is easy to cut up and eat as people attending such affairs are often middle-aged or elderly, with teeth not as strong as they were. I remember a Royal Garden Party where a complete set of false teeth buried in a macaroon was found behind a bush . . .

Anyone setting about this mousse will be relieved to find it has been scaled down to serve six rather than six hundred:

4 eggs, 6 oz caster sugar, 2 large lemons, ¼ pint water, ½ oz powdered gelatine (a slightly rounded tablespoon), ¼ pint double cream.

Separate the eggs and yolks. To the yolks, add the sugar and finely grated rind of one lemon. Strain the juice of both lemons and set aside. Measure the water into a saucepan and sprinkle in the gelatine; allow it to soak for a few minutes then place over a low heat and stir until dissolved but do not boil. Cream the yolks, sugar and rind and when thoroughly mixed, add the hot melted gelatine, pouring in very gradually and stirring all the time. Put this mixture in a cool place and whisk from time to time until it thickens. When the mixture is thick but not yet set, whip the egg whites until stiff and fold them into the cream mixture. Chill until firm. Whip the double cream and spoon it lightly over the surface of the mousse. Decorate if liked with a little grated plain chocolate and chill until serving.

CLEMENT FREUD

EMERGENCY RATIONS

I reckon that a well-designed kitchen should not only have the standard spiceshelf, refrigerator, liquidiser and rubbish-bin. Somewhere, tucked unobtrusively in a corner, there ought to be an emergency larder.

This should cater for three eventualities:

Firstly, disenchantment by people who have been fed ... like children who were less than enthusiastic about the pheasant kedgeree; unexpected vegetarians, followers of McRobiot and other kinks.

For them there should be unequivocal goodies: Heinz tomato soup. Salted almonds. Boxes of fudge. Packets of Jaffa Cakes. Slabs of Cadbury's milk and nut. Crunchie bars. San Pellegrino orangeade. Tins of Chivers raspberries. Peppermint Matchmakers.

The second shelf of the larder should house foodstuffs designed to upgrade meals ... to be used for such eventualities as rich uncles dropping in or the discovery that the man you thought was just another of your daughter's boyfriends is also Parliamentary Secretary to the Department of Environment dealing with the proposed demolition of your house.

You need tins of lobster bisque and turtle soup. Real *pâté de foie gras*. A jar of smoked cods' roe. Bath Oliver biscuits. A duck in curaçao. Bottles of fruit in brandy. Escoffier Sauce Robert and Sauce Cumberland. Tins of mushrooms and asparagus tips. Miniatures of liqueur. A potted Stilton. Items all that can elevate to a three-course feast the cheese and biscuits you were intending to munch. Grilled lamb cutlets will shine under a Cumberland Sauce. Open the tin of duck and slice the breast across slivers of toast for a starter.

The final part of the store should cater for the occasions when you bring home half a dozen people – at least two of whom, you were pretty certain, were taking you out to a meal. This section of provisions must be long-lasting on the basis that it may never happen. What you do is think of a staggeringly simple, totally delicious menu which is based entirely on tins but make sure that you always have butter, cream and one or two other essentials of the good life in your refrigerator.

CHRISTOPHER FRY

A DELICIOUS CHICKEN LIVER PÂTÉ TO KEEP YOU ALERT

To ward off sleepiness in the afternoon what is better for the midday meal than a little chicken liver pâté on toast? My wife, a splendid cook, puts about half-a-pound of chicken livers in a casserole dish, with an equal quantity of butter, herbs and chopped up onion (no clove of garlic for me!). After an hour and a half in a moderate oven Regulo 5 (375°), pour off some of the butter and mince the rest of the ingredients (or whizz them in a blender). Leave to cool in a dish and then cover with the melted butter remaining. Refrigerate if possible until eating time.

It may have been the recipe used by Margaret in *The Lady's Not for Burning* with her goose liver, but not the reason for her party starting so disastrously:

'Goose liver,
Cold larks, cranberry tarts and sucking pig,
And now everyone looks as though they only
Wanted to eat each other, which might in the circumstances
Be the best possible thing.'

ROGER FULFORD

WHEATGERM CASSEROLE BREAD

3 breakfast cups of plain flour, ½ cup wheatgerm, 2 teaspoons salt, 1 tablespoon dry yeast, 2 oz soft margarine, 2 tablespoons molasses, 1⅓ cup very hot water.

Mix the flour, salt, wheatgerm and yeast. Beat in the margarine. Gradually add the water and molasses and beat for two minutes in an electric blender. Check the mixture and add enough flour to make sure of a thick batter. Beat a further two minutes and add more flour if necessary.

Cover and put to rise in a warm place for about 45 minutes. This should double the bulk of the batter. Stir it down well and turn into a casserole.

Bake for about 45 minutes at Regulo 5 (375°).

ROY FULLER

WAGNER'S *GINGERBREAD*

For a long time I have been an enthusiastic but lazy and therefore non-regular maker of bread and cakes. The cake recipe I have used most during the last five years is for what has become known in my family as 'Wagner's Gingerbread'.

It appeared in a BBC publication of 1972 (sent to me, with more weighty papers, in my capacity as BBC Governor) called *The Fourth Jimmy Young Cook Book* – recipes submitted by listeners and broadcast by Mr Young on Radio 1. This cheap and easy recipe came from Mrs Julie Barr of Brockley, SE4. She got it from her mother, who used it when she worked for the composer Richard Wagner. Wagner died in 1883, so the recipe is of respectable antiquity. It follows here. I have very slightly amended ingredients and method to accord with my own experience and moderate food-crankiness.

3 breakfast cups wholemeal (plain) flour, ½ lb poly-unsaturated marge, 1 breakfast cup caster sugar, 2 teaspoons baking powder, 2 teaspoons bicarbonate of soda, 2 teaspoons ground ginger, 1 breakfast cup syrup, 1½ breakfast cups boiling water.

Grease and line a tin, *not* with a loose bottom, of about 8 in diameter and 2½ in depth (or equivalent other shape). Heat oven to Regulo 5 (375°). Needless to say, an oven thermometer will be required to check the vagaries of our rotten natural gas. Rub the marge into the flour and add the rest of the dry ingredients. Add the syrup – which will probably need warming first. Most of the syrup adhering to the cup will be washed out by the boiling water, which add next. (The boiling water is the secret of success, Mrs Barr commented.)

Mix thoroughly – saves washing up to use the metal tablespoon previously required for dealing with the syrup. Do not be alarmed at the liquidity of the mixture but pour it into the prepared tin and bake on the middle shelf at the stated temperature for 1½ hours. The result should be moist, light and extremely edible. This is probably the *'herrlicher Kuchen'* (splendid cake) offered by David to Hans Sachs as a birthday present at the start of Act III of *Die Meistersinger*!

DAVID GARNETT

A FEW SOPHISTICATED DISHES

The best food is that which one has grown or gathered oneself. Vegetables young and fresh from one's own garden, field and wood mushrooms one has collected, fruit that one has picked, fish that one has caught, pheasants, grouse and hares that one has shot. This is for most of us, usually impossible. But at least one should aim at eating the food of the country one is living in and in the freshest state – not out of a deep freeze, but each in its season.

I live in France without a vegetable garden and how I regret the green spears of asparagus with a thick mayonnaise to which one had incorporated a spoonful of red wine and a squeeze of lemon, the first strawberries and raspberries and best of all red and white currants, carefully strigged and powdered with caster sugar, looking like a dish of pearls and rubies. Then the first new potatoes which one has scratched out, without sacrificing the plant, boiled with mint. Then the field mushrooms and blewits and blackberries from the hedges and whortleberries from the woods.

Here I get globe artichokes and melons they grow in the fields, various kinds of fungi and delicious wild cherry-plums.

But I can recommend a few more sophisticated dishes.

CRAB AND AVOCADO SALAD

Remove all the brown, red and white meat from the body and claws of a good heavy dry crab, being careful to throw away the gills. Mix with the flesh of two perfectly ripe avocados – with no bruised or brown flesh. Dress with olive oil, wine vinegar with a spoonful of red wine and a teaspoon of French mustard, salt and pepper beaten up. You can amalgamate a salad of cabbage lettuce hearts if you wish.

CUTTLEFISH AND AUBERGINES

Slice aubergine on the slant, salt each piece and leave to drain for an hour. Clean the cuttlefish removing beak, bone and intestines and cut up in pieces about 2 in long. Wash and dry the slices of aubergines when they have drained and fry them in oil until soft. Add the cuttlefish and cook till they turn white. Put in a closed earthen casserole with a sliced tomato. Season with pepper. Add bay leaf and bouquet d'herbes.

Cover in red wine and stew gently in the oven for 3 hours. See it doesn't dry up. You can use squid too for this dish, but I prefer cuttlefish with a white bone to squid with a transparent one.

PIG'S TROTTER

This is one of the cheapest and best dishes.

Buy a whole trotter – not split in two.

Boil it in water with a bay leaf or two, peppercorns and juniper berries if you have them, until you can easily remove the bones. Take all the flesh off the bones and put the bones back in the liquid and boil them for stock – which will set in a firm jelly – for soup.

When the flesh has grown cold and set, dip in egg and bread crumbs and fry until hot.

MRS GASKELL

MISS BARKER'S SUPPER PARTY

Another tray! 'Oh, gentility!' thought I, 'can you endure this last shock?' For Miss Barker had ordered (nay, I doubt not, prepared, although she did say: 'Why, Peggy, what have you brought us?' and looked pleasantly surprised at the unexpected pleasure) all sorts of good things for supper – scalloped oysters, potted lobsters, jelly, a dish called 'little Cupids' (which was in great favour with the Cranford ladies, although too expensive to be given, except on solemn and state occasions – macaroons sopped in brandy, I should have called it, if I had not known its more refined and classical name). In short, we were evidently to be feasted with all that was sweetest and best; and we thought it better to submit graciously, even at the cost of our gentility – which never ate suppers in general, but which, like most non-supper-eaters, was particularly hungry on all special occasions.

Miss Barker, in her former sphere, had, I dare say, been made acquainted with the beverage they call cherry-brandy. We none of us had ever seen such a thing, and rather shrank back when she proffered it us – 'just a little, leetle glass, ladies; after the oysters and lobsters, you know. Shellfish are sometimes thought not very wholesome.' We all shook our heads like female mandarins; but, at last, Mrs Jamieson suffered herself to be persuaded, and we followed her lead. It was not exactly unpalatable, though so hot and so strong that we thought ourselves bound to give evidence that we were not accustomed to such things by coughing terribly – almost as strangely as Miss Barker had done, before we were admitted by Peggy.

'It's very strong,' said Miss Pole, as she put down her empty glass; 'I do believe there's spirit in it.'

'Only a little drop – just necessary to make it keep,' said Miss Barker. 'You know we put brandy-pepper over our preserves to make them keep. I often feel tipsy myself from eating damson tart.'

WILLIAM GERHARDIE

DINNER WITH SYLVIA

Sylvia wanted chicken. There were two kinds of chicken. A whole chicken cost 500 roubles. A wing, 100 roubles. The rate of exchange, be it remembered, at that time was only 200 roubles to £1 sterling. The enormous head waiter strongly recommended the whole chicken. 'Straight from Paris in an aeroplane,' he said. I felt cold in the feet.

Sylvia hesitated dangerously. 'I don't think I want as much as a whole chicken. I'll have a wing,' she uttered at last. I breathed freely.

'But the wing is larger than the chicken, madam,' said the fiend. I longed to ask him to explain that curious mathematical perversion, but a latent sense of gallantry deterred me. I felt like clubbing him. But civilisation suffered me to go on suffering in silence. '*Go away*,' I whispered inwardly. '*Oh, go away!*' But I sat still, resigned. Only my left eyelid began to twitch a little nervously.

'All right,' she said. 'I'll have the whole chicken, then.'

Five hundred roubles! £2 10s for a solitary chicken! My dead grandfather raised his bushy eyebrows. And I already pictured to myself how under the removed restraints of matrimony, probably in my braces and shirt-sleeves, I would exhort my wife to cut down her criminal expenditure.

There was a variety of ice-creams at 'popular prices', but Sylvia ordered a silly dish called 'Pêche Melba' – and proportionately more expenseive.

'What wine, darling?'

'French,' she said.

'But what kind?'

'White, darling.'

The waiter bent over the wine list and pointed to the figures which were double those he did not point to.

'But what kind?'

'Sweet. The sweetest.'

And, according to the waiter, the sweetest wine concorded with the highest figure on the list.

How I hate extravagant drinks! How I hate extravagant food! What I really wanted now, if I could have my way, was eggs and bacon and hot milk.

'Yes, that will do,' she said.

The waiter, bowing, whipped his napkin under the arm and retired with the air of one who has his work cut out. The band struck up a gay waltz, but in my soul was darkness.

ROBERT GITTINGS

BOSTON BACON AND BAKED BEANS

I first tasted this at the Boston Tennis and Racquet Club, where my American publisher, the poet Peter Davison at Atlantic Little-Brown, kindly managed to get me membership, while I was teaching at Boston University and working on a book. Another kind New England friend, also a poet obtained the recipe, and I now regularly enjoy this dish, which is cheap and in other ways greatly appreciated by poets. The recipe below will provide a splendidly filling meal for eight struggling verse-makers.

Soak 1 lb haricot beans overnight, simmer until soft and keep water, cut up ½ lb bacon, mix 1 cup black molasses, 1 chopped onion, 1 teaspoon salt, pepper, mustard.

Layer beans, bacon, and molasses-mix in large brown pot; then cover with bean water. Bake at Regulo ½ (250°) for 6 hours, last hour uncovered.

Max.

GILES GORDON

HAGGIS

Haggis three times a year is sufficient. I am not a member of the Scottish Nationalist Party but I *enjoy* the taste of haggis. My mother, who lives in Edinburgh (but is Irish) sends us (my wife is English) a haggis from the great Edinburgh butcher McSween on three dates of the year: for Burns' Nicht, St Andrew's Day and Hogmanay. We have it boiled, and if there's any left over, fried the next day. Haggis is traditionally eaten with mashed tatties and neeps. Being a heretic, I prefer it with fried potatoes. The texture of haggis, mashed tatties and neeps is, for my palate, too lacking in variation whereas the contrast of spicy and crisp fried potatoes is most stimulating.

No two cooks or butchers make haggis identically but for the do-it-yourself fanatic *Chambers's* (as it used to be spelt) *Dictionary* acknowledges to the following ingredients: the heart, lungs and liver of a sheep, calf, etc (etc!), chopped up with suet, onions, oatmeal, etc, seasoned and boiled in a sheep's stomach bag. Obviously the secret of haggis is less what derives from the sheep or the calf or other Scotch animal than the etcetera.

Those who are afraid of haggis are either those who haven't eaten it, or who have had served up to them an indifferent one.

EDWARD GOREY

MR EARBRASS STARTS A NOVEL

On November 18th of alternate years Mr Earbrass begins writing 'his new novel'. Weeks ago he chose its title from a list of them he keeps in a little green notebook. It being teatime of the 17th, he is alarmed not to have thought of a plot to which *The Unstrung Harp* might apply, but his mind will keep reverting to the last biscuit on the plate.

Edward Gorey

HARRY GRAHAM

ADVICE ON INVITATIONS TO TEA AND THEIR REFUSAL

Example:

Mrs A.B.C. presents
Her respects and compliments
To Mrs and Miss D.
She would deem it very pleasant
If the latter could be present
At her tiny tea.
(Note: There will be Bridge for those who care to take a hand,
Tennis in the garden and a military band.)

Reply:

Mrs and Miss D. express
Their eternal gratefulness
To Mrs A.B.C.
Tennis they've no time to spare for,
Tea is not a meal they care for,
Bridge they never play.
Military bands for them have little fascination,
So they must reluctantly refuse her invitation.

WINSTON GRAHAM

GOLF STEW

When I am working I like to play golf about three times a week. I play nine to twelve holes, nearly always on my own, and I scarcely ever speak to anyone. When I come home it is time for lunch, and one of my favourite meals in the cold weather is my wife's version of Irish stew, with a bottle of Worthington.

For the stew she buys six cutlets of middle neck of lamb and three pieces of best end of lamb. This she puts on the previous day to simmer gently in water for two hours. Next day she takes off all the fat that has come to the surface, and adds one large swede, one carrot, one parsnip, six–eight leeks all sliced, one bay leaf and two teaspoons of salt. She allows this to simmer for a further two hours, then adds six potatoes and three slices of smoked back bacon. When these are cooked the dish is ready for serving. This is enough for four to six people according to the size of appetite.

BENNY GREEN

When Ira Gershwin first began writing a lyric for his brother George's melody of *I Got Rythm*, he composed a 'dummy' lyric to help him keep the melody in his head. This dummy is a stern warning to all who like food. Sing to the tune of *I Got Rhythm*:

Roly poly, eating solely, ravioli,
Better watch your diet or bust.
Lunch or dinner, you're a sinner, please get thinner,
Losing all that fat is a must.

GRAHAM GREENE

GUESSING THE WEIGHT OF THE CAKE

He had always liked cakes, especially rich Dundees and dark brown home-made fruit cakes tasting elusively of Guinness. He said to the lady at the stall, 'You won't think me greedy if I have another sixpennyworth?'

'No. Please.'

'I should say, then, four pounds eight and a half ounces.'

He was conscious of an odd silence, as if all the afternoon they had been waiting for just this, but hadn't somehow expected it from him. Then a stout woman who hovered on the outskirts gave a warm and hearty laugh. 'Lawks,' she said. 'Anybody can tell you're a bachelor.'

'As a matter of fact,' the lady behind the stall rebuked her sharply, 'this gentleman has won. He is not more than a fraction of an ounce out. That counts,' she said, with nervous whimsicality, 'as a direct hit.'

'Four pounds eight ounces,' the stout woman said. 'Well, you be careful, that's all. It'll be as heavy as lead.'

'On the contrary, it's made with real eggs.'

The stout woman went away laughing ironically in the direction of the clothing stall.

JOYCE GRENFELL

Oh! I'd like to have a pickin'
Of a little bit of chicken
And a little bit of tongue
And a little bit of ham;
And if I was a good 'un
Of a little bit of puddun
And a little bit of tart
And strawberry jam.

(Taught me by my pa when I was very small. After he died I found a copy of it in his hand with a note to say: 'Taught me by a boatman on Loch Rannoch at the turn of the century.')

JANE GRIGSON

TRIPES À LA LYONNAISE

A more lively version of tripe and onions.

Equal weight of tripe and onions, water to cover the tripe, an extra onion stuck with four cloves, carrots, celery, leeks, bouquet garni, salt and pepper, a beaten egg, breadcrumbs, butter.

Buy your tripe ready blanched; if not, you will have to scald it and soak it for three hours in cold water with a dash of vinegar. Then blanch it for a good half-hour in boiling, salted water.

Cook it for two hours in the water flavoured with vegetables, seasoning and herbs. Peel and slice the onions (except the onion stuck with cloves, which is used in the bouillon), and sauté them gently in the butter until they are cooked and golden. Keep them warm. Do not cook the onions until the tripe is ready and drained. Cut the tripe into squares, dip them in the beaten egg, then in the crumbs and fry in butter until they are crisp. This can be done in the butter left from frying the onions. Put the tripe pieces on top of the onions, swill the buttery pan round with some wine vinegar and pour it over the tripe. Sprinkle the top with chopped parsley and serve the dish very hot, with very hot plates.

GEORGE AND WEEDON GROSSMITH

DINNER FOR MR HARDFUR HUTTLE

May 10th. Received a letter from Mr Franching, of Peckham, asking us to dine with him tonight, at seven o'clock, to meet Mr Hardfur Huttle, a very clever writer for the American papers. Franching apologised for the short notice; but said he had at the last moment been disappointed of two of his guests and regarded us as old friends who would not find filling up the gap. Carrie rather demurred at the invitation; but I explained to her that Franching was very well off and influential, and we could not afford to offend him. 'And we are sure to get a good dinner and a good glass of champagne.' 'Which never agrees with you!' Carrie replied sharply, I regarded Carrie's observation as unsaid. Mr Franching asked us to wire a reply. As he had said nothing about dress in the letter, I wired back: 'With pleasure. Is it full dress?' and by leaving out our name, just got the message within the sixpence.

Got back early to give time to dress, which we received a telegram instructing us to do. I wanted Carrie to meet me at Franching's house; but she would not do so, so I had to go home to fetch her. What a long journey it is from Holloway to Peckham!

Why do people live such a long way off? Having to change buses, I allowed plenty of time – in fact, too much; for we arrived at twenty minutes to seven, and Franching, so the servant said, had only just gone up to dress. However, he was down as the clock struck seven; he must have dressed very quickly.

I must say it was quite a distinguished party, and although we did not know anybody personally, they all seemed to be quite swells. Franching had got a professional waiter, and evidently spared no expense. There were flowers on the table round some fairy-lamps, and the effect, I must say, was exquisite. The wine was good and there was plenty of champagne, concerning which Franching said he, himself, never wished to taste better. We were ten in number, and a *menu* card to each. One lady said she always preserved the *menu* and got the guests to write their names on the back.

We all of us followed her example, except Mr Huttle, who was of course the important guest.

The dinner-party consisted of Mr Franching, Mr Hardfur Huttle, Mr and Mrs Samuel Hillbutter, Mrs Field, Mr and Mrs Purdick, Mr Pratt, Mr R. Kent, and, last, but not least, Mr and Mrs Charles Pooter. Franching said he was sorry he had no lady for me to take in to dinner. I replied that I preferred it, which I afterwards thought was a very uncomplimentary observation to make.

I sat next to Mrs Field at dinner. She seemed a well-informed lady, but was very deaf. It did not much matter, for Mr Hardfur Huttle did all the talking. He is a marvellously intellectual man and says things which from other people would seem quite alarming. How I wish I could remember even a quarter of his brilliant conversation. I made a few little reminding notes on the *menu* card.

KATHLEEN HALE

STEAMED PRAWNS

These make a good and unusual light supper. You can use fresh or frozen prawns but avoid the tinned variety and choose the biggest size you can. With rice, this recipe will serve two or three people.

Dust about 1 lb shelled prawns with cornflour. Place them in a dish to fit within a steamer or over a saucepan (but in this case bear in mind that you will have to seal the saucepan securely). Slice a few spring onions, 4 oz mushrooms and 4 oz cucumber and add to the prawns. Season with fresh black pepper and add ½ glass white wine and a couple of tablespoons soya sauce. Seal the steamer well and cook over a few inches of boiling water until tender – about 8 minutes.

ALEX HAMILTON

OX-TAIL

One day I am downing rock-salmon, with gusto in Clerkenwell; the next I am disparaging your actual smoked Nordic-lax-type salmon Chez Bocuse near Armagnac, and complaining that the finger-bowls are late. One day I am contentedly on White Shield at the Betsey Trotwood (Butchers Arms as was) – the most verbal brew I know; the next I am watching them bottle Noilly Prat in Marseillan, and hearing how the local churches serve aperitifs at Mass. One day I write for ten hours promising myself a shrivelled Burmese cheroot if I meet my deadline; the next I am in the Partagas factory itself in Havana, sneering at anything under nine inches, hand-rolled. This is what it is to be a travelling palate. If you write for a paper your stomach is not your own. And in the great houses, when the veal paprika is so tender as to excite pity, it is a solecism to ask for the recipe. So I'll recommend nothing exotic, but with the firm belief that writers of all kinds should lay on extra weight whenever they can, against the hard times, suggest that one good ox-tail (yellow fat means cow) is worth a thousand words. Trimmed, it should weigh about two-and-a-half pounds. You can cut the vertebrae with a penknife if you have the knock – otherwise ask your butcher (and see if he has the knack). It's always cheaper in summer than winter. Boil unsalted till almost cooked, then de-fat. Put in casserole, add onions, tomatoes, turnips, barley and a bay leaf. Now salt and pepper. Cover. Cook in a moderate oven for one-and-a-half hours. Tail stands a lot of cooking, but take out before it falls off the bone.

I'm in favour of rice and Burgundy with it, especially when writing a novel of sex and violence.

IRENE HANDL

OYSTERS AND JELLIED EELS

My favourite food is oysters, indubitably. Colchesters, served on their deep shell married up with thin brown bread and butter, lemons (freshly cut halves, none of those niggardly, wilting sections), coarse grey pepper and, for the lucky, a deliciously cool, white wine. I'm only allowed draught lager, but I'm not complaining. It's the price of oysters I worry about. I once consumed four dozen of these princely bi-valves without winking and I hope to again when one of my books is made into a film. Until then, here is a dish I'm very fond of – a posh version of jellied eels which makes a good first course. It's simple to make and can be prepared in advance because it keeps well.

You need 2 lb eels cut into 2-in sections and skinned (any good fishmonger *used* to do this for you). You'll also need a carrot, an onion, a clove of garlic, a dozen of pepper corns, salt, a bay leaf, a small piece of nutmeg or blade of mace, a lemon, a strip of lemon peel and a small bunch of parsley.

Stew everything apart from the lemon with half a glass of white wine in a heavy, covered pan. When the eel is tender lift the pieces out with a straining spoon and arrange them neatly on a good looking dish – earthenware or heavy old china looks best.

Strain the liquor, saving the carrot which you'll need for garnishing, and pour into a clean saucepan. Correct the seasoning and add the juice of a lemon. Heat but do not bring to the boil.

Melt the contents of a packet of gelatin with a little of the hot liquor and add to the rest of the liquor. Stir well and allow to cool until tepid.

Strain the liquor over the fish (there should be about a pint) and when nearly set, decorate the dish with rounds of carrot and a couple of bay leaves. When quite cold, cover the dish with foil and chill until wanted. Serve with lemon sections and freshly cut brown bread and butter.

DOROTHY HARTLEY

PARSNIP CAKES

Parsnip Cakes are delicious. The parsnip was our earliest English nep (all roots were 'neps' – tur nep, pars nep, etc.) the potato came into favour because 'it was a sweet roote which faree exceedeth our English parsnep'.

Boil the parnsips, and, when cooked, mash them very thoroughly, working in a small quantity of flour, a good pinch of mace, pepper and salt, and a large lump of butter or dripping. Form into round flat cakes, about an inch through. Egg and breadcrumb them, pressing well, and fry in smoking fat until brown. They should be crisp outside, and open to a soft golden cream inside.

For a really good winter-evening supper, take a couple of brown and creamy parsnip cakes, a couple of fried tomatoes, hot brown gravy, and brussels sprouts.

JON HARTRIDGE
also Literary Editor of the *Oxford Mail*

PHILLY CHEESECAKE

Chaps are supposed, like Desperate Dan and his cow pie, to drool over massive savouries, pungent, weighty, thick with flavour. It's dishes like *steak au poivre,* roast beef with Yorkshire pud, cold game pie or Madras curried chicken with dal that are supposed to have man-appeal.

And there's no denying that they appeal to this man. There's a considerable range of main course dishes that occupy the top shelf in his mental larder. They issue invitations that are so uniformly tempting that it would be unjust if not hurtful to pick a favourite.

But there's no doubt about what's my favourite pud. It's one my wife makes when she's feeling indulgent . . .

Base: 8 oz digestive biscuits, 4 oz melted butter.
Topping: ½ pint double cream, ½ teaspoon vanilla essence, 6 oz Philadelphia cream cheese, 4 oz sugar, a 14 oz tin of blackcurrant or cherry pie filling.

Crush the biscuits and mix well with the melted butter. Press down well into a cake tin with a removable base. Whip the cream and vanilla essence until just stiff. In another bowl, whip cheese with sugar until creamy. Combine the two with a large spoon. Spread the mixture on the biscuit base and chill for half an hour. Pour over the contents of the tin of blackcurrant or cherry filling and chill until serving. To serve, remove from tin to flat plate.

JAMES HERRIOT

PANNACCLETY

I am still devoted to the simple dishes of my Scottish upbringing like mince and tatties and mutton pie and chips, but one childish joy remains with me now, and my wife cooks it for me when she is too busy for other things, knowing that her peculiar husband will enjoy it better than a banquet.

It springs from the north-east of England where I was born. It is called 'pannacclety'. I'll put it in caps: PANNACCLETY. Or that's what they call it in Sunderland, anyway. I have also heard it called PAN HAGERTY and other things and it used to be the food of the poor in the north-east.

It is based on the humble potato, sliced quite thinly and cooked in water in a big frying-pan or baking-tin along with bacon and onions. That's all, but it is heavenly.

All sorts of people used to eat it in Sunderland – maybe they still do – on occasions when they had to whip up something quick, tasty and nourishing. I had a dear old auntie in Sunderland who cooked it on washing day. I used to wake up and hear the poss-stick (ever heard of that?) bashing away at the clothes and lying there, as a small boy, I used to think 'there'll be pannacclety today' and there always was.

CHRISTOPHER HIBBERT

BEEF BURGUNDY

Ingredients: 3 lb topside beef, flour, 5 tablespoons butter, 4 tablespoons olive oil, $\frac{1}{2}$ lb green bacon, 5 tablespoons cognac, $\frac{1}{2}$ bottle Burgundy, beef stock, sugar, salt, black pepper, lemon juice, 2 chopped leeks, 2 chopped carrots, 5 chopped shallots, chopped Spanish onion, 20 button onions, 10 button mushrooms, chopped clove of garlic, bouquet garni, chopped parsley.

Heat 2 tablespoons each butter and olive oil in a frying-pan. Sauté bacon until crisp and transfer to a large casserole. Add the remaining oil and butter to the pan and brown the cubed beef, previously rolled in flour. Season, flambé with the warmed cognac and transfer to the casserole. Leaving aside the onion, brown the vegetables in the pan and add them to the casserole.

Add the bouquet garni, stock and wine to cover the meat and vegetables. Cover the casserole and cook slowly for an hour or so then stir in a tablespoon of butter mixed with a tablespoon of flour. Cook for a further couple of hours until the meat is tender. Brown the onion in butter with some sugar in a saucepan and add a cupful of wine. Cover and cook on a low heat then add a little lemon juice. Add this mixture to the contents of the casserole, remove the bouquet garni and serve with parsley and mashed potatoes.

PATRICIA HIGHSMITH

CORNBREAD DRESSING

I love Cornbread Dressing, called stuffing by some. This is for turkeys or chickens, but not ducks. You bake a piepan of cornbread in the usual manner*, then remove it from pan, put in big salad bowl, break it up with the fingers and mix an egg in (raw). Add nearly a cup of diced raw onion, another such measure of diced celery including green leaves; touch of sage if preferred, or enjoyed.

Extra salt – assuming cornbread already has some. Stuff the fowl with this, then bake the fowl. Greedy consumers like me bake extra batch of cornbread, treat the same way with egg, celery, etc, then return to oven to bake in piepan and baste it occasionally with juice from the roasting fowl. Delicious hot or cold seems to improve the next day or day after, cut in wedges. Quite rich and divine. I speak with nostalgia, because I can't always get the cornbread now I live in France, so it is a rare thing for me.

* (For those of us who have never baked cornbread, 'usual manner' or not, the following recipe might be useful):

Mix a tablespoon of dry yeast with a cup of tepid water and 3 tablespoons of honey. Stand for 5 minutes. Add 2 tablespoons of olive oil and 2 beaten eggs. Sift a cup of yellow cornmeal, ⅓ cup of oat flour (use finely milled oats), 2 tablespoons wheatgerm, ½ cup powdered milk and a teaspoon of salt into a bowl and pour on the liquid. Combine them briefly and pour the batter into a hot, lightly-greased oven pan. Bake for about 25 minutes at Regulo 7 (425°).

THOMAS HINDE

THE WEDDING PIE

Twenty-five years ago in a beach restaurant near Lecce in the heel of Italy my wife and I became briefly sucked – I think that is the right word – into a wedding feast.

It was one of those family parties where about twenty people of ages varying from a month to eighty years, from at least four generations, were sitting at a single vast table. The glossy pall of plastic prosperity had not then descended on Italy and there was little finery and a good deal of greying stubble on display. They were a fishing family, I think. I remember little else about the occasion except the central dish.

This came in a huge pottery casserole, in which, it seemed, everything from mussels, winkles, cockles, squid, crab and lobster to eggs, bacon, courgette, aubergine, sweet pepper and cheese had been baked with about a gallon of olive oil into a gargantuan purple pie. I certainly can't call this my favourite dish because, in the terminology of today, I suppose it would be a 'one-off'. But it was probably my most memorable.

Though now I come to think of it there is just possibly another reason why it has remained in my mind. About twelve hours later I came up in raised white patches, a quarter of an inch deep and many inches across, over the whole of my body, and the same happened to my wife soon afterwards. We spent the next five days writhing and vomiting in a fourth-class hotel with a single Asian-type lavatory and basket for the paper. Our illness was of course caused by eating too many of the infected melons which stand in golden mountains about the pavements of Lecce. I would never suggest that anything more than coincidence connects it with that great wedding pie.

ERIC HISCOCK

ROASTED-IN-FOIL POUSSIN

My mother used to say: 'Anyone can cook if they have got the materials.' Materials were a wee bit lacking in the house where I was born, but we managed somehow. Things like breast of lamb stuffed with something cheap, bolstered up with lots of potatoes that father grew on an allotment in Oxford's Osney. Things are a bit better now, and as a loner I can experiment providing I've typed enough words each week to buy stuff like asparagus, avocado pears, a slice or two of smoked salmon and a tin of John Lusty's admirable turtle soup. Add a bottle of Reserve du Patron burgundy from ElVino's and you've got a meal. But my favourite dish is poussin done in silver foil for 40 minutes in a fairly hot oven at Regulo 4 (350°).

Take a single poussin, insert garlic cloves, half a Spanish onion, a walnut-sized lump of butter, lots of pepper, some salt, then cover the bird with butter and any fat you may have kept from a chicken, pheasant, or turkey that has been left after roasting. Enclose the whole in silver foil (well sealed so that the fat when hot cannot escape into the roasting-pan) and leave in the oven for 30 of the 40 minutes necessary to bring the dish to perfection. Ten minutes before serving, open the foil, exposing the poussin, and baste with the now hot and melted covering of fat. That will brown the breast. The result should be delicious and more than enough for one. Nothing more than a tossed green salad is needed. Wash it all down with a bottle of fairly good claret, say a Moûton Cadet bottled in France by Rothschild. If you are entertaining, double the poussin. The lovely thing about such entertaining is that you can leave the dish alone and concentrate on your guests.

DAVID HOLLOWAY
Also Literary Editor of the *Daily Telegraph*

I am a left-over guzzler, and I glory in being one. The guzzler is one who may be found haunting kitchens and larders where left-overs may be found – steak and kidney pies grown cold with the gravy solidified into splendid jelly, spaghetti bolognaise grown glutinous so that pasta and sauce may be picked up together, quiches firmly set that may be cut off in thin slices again and again. There are always bits inaccessible to the carving knife that may be picked off the carcase of a bird by knowledgeable fingers, while hacking at a joint yields treasure, and there is always the marrow to be had from the mutton bone. The prerequisite for good guzzling is good cooking. In my case, I have a wife deeply concerned that there is not enough food to go round. There always is, and enough for the guzzler too, even if it is only the residue in the gravy-boat. Like any scavenger the guzzler has his virtues – no food to throw away – but he can be a menace. Left-overs may well furnish another meal and a plate of steak and kidney put aside for another occasion looks less than appetising when it is a pock-marked relic after the pieces of kidney have neatly been winkled out.

MICHAEL HOLROYD

AFTERNOON NAP TEA

This dish is best prepared in the early afternoon. When 'Woman's Hour' fades into 'Listen with Mother', approach the kitchen. Put some water on to boil and while it is heating prepare a tray with cup, saucer and spoon, milk, sugar and a tea bag. Pour the boiling water into a thermos flask, screw on the cap and remove to the tray. Carry this tray to the bedside. Switch on 'Afternoon Theatre' . . .

When you wake up, flop the tea bag into the flask, replace cap on thermos, doze for three or four more minutes, then pour: a fine dish of tea, to taste.

Credit where it's due: I have adapted this menu from Miss Louise Davies, BSc, Head of the Geriatric Nutrition Unit, whose illustrated recipes are recommended by the Emeritus Professor of Queen Elizabeth College as overcoming some of the problems that face elderly, as well as literary, people.

JAN HOPCRAFT

QUICK HONEY ICE-CREAM

Unusual and delicious for a dinner party ending, you'll need 4 oz of honey, ½ teaspoon ground ginger, 4 eggs, ½ pint double cream and pieces of crystallised ginger for decoration.

Separate the whites from the yolks and whip together the yolks, honey, ground ginger and cream until the mixture thickens.

Whip the whites to peaks and fold them into the cream mixture. Put the mixture in a suitable container and into the ice-making compartment of a refrigerator or into a deep freezer. To keep the ice-cream smooth, turn the crystals with a fork just as it is beginning to set (about an hour after placing it in the freezer). Serve sprinkled with chopped crystallised ginger. (*Serves 4 to 6.*)

BARRY HUMPHRIES
After consultation with Dame Edna Everidge

EDNAWICHES

Sandwich fillings need not be dull, for Australia has pioneered some delicious and exotic sambie*-centres. When making sambies remember that in most cases they have to travel a long way in hot little boxes before they get gobbled up for lunch. There's nothing worse, is there readers, than a horrid dry crumbly sambie? So, remember my Golden Rule and use the moistest possible ingredients. Here is a particularly tasty filling as a lunch-hour thrill for kiddies and senior citizens alike:

1 sweet eating apple, 2 snowballs (to be bought at any lolly shop), slices of bread.

Peel and core the sweet apple. Cut into thin slices, *taking care that there is no taint of onion on your chopping board.* Spread on to thin slices of buttered white bread. Cut snowballs into thin slices and spread above apple, cover with another slice of buttered bread, and stick sandwich firmly together by hand, *taking care that there is no taint of onion on the palm.* (Garlic is also a non-desirable odour to invade this dish. Not even New Australians would think that nice.)

* 'Sambies' – an increasingly popular diminutive for 'sandwiches'. Variant: 'Sambos'.

HAMMOND INNES

COQUILLES DE SALSIFIS

If you are lucky enough, as we are, to have a garden that produces vegetables in season all the year round, then you are at least part way to being vegetarians, since the dishes, particularly the soups, are so fresh and delicate in flavour. In March, which is about the most difficult month for vegetables in England, we can still call upon more than a dozen straight from the ground. One of the best is salsify, 'the vegetable oyster', which really is something like oysters. As with so many dishes, it is the sauce that gives it perfection. My wife, Dorothy, has her own version and the result is superb.

Wash the salsify very carefully and scrape off black skin. Put immediately in water with lemon juice. Cut them either into little finger-pieces or into rounds, and cook in boiling water with salt and lemon juice until just tender – about 15 minutes. Drain them and, for perfection, fry them a few minutes in butter, but this is not necessary. Meanwhile, make a sauce, starting with a butter and flour roux, using for liquid about three-quarters water the salsify was cooked in, to one quarter top of milk, or cream. Add a very little finely grated cheese, salt, pepper, a little nutmeg. Bear in mind the thing you want to taste in the end is the salsify!

Pour a little sauce in each scallop-shell, making sure it is as smooth as cream, and the same consistency as double cream. Then fill the shells with the salsify, and mix with it a few slices of hard-boiled egg. Remember to leave room for the sauce to cover the salsify and egg. Finally, sprinkle a little crumbled crisp bacon over the sauce in each scallop-shell. All this can be done in advance. Just before you want to eat them, put them in the oven or under a grill until just lightly browned and bubbly. You can sprinkle a little parsley over just before serving and offer sections of lemon to squeeze.

LAURENCE IRVING

LA GOURMANDISE D'UN LITTÉRATEUR FRUSTRÉ

Authors provide the very bread
On which the livelihood of publishers depends
(Several of whom it must be said
Have been among my closest friends.)
But times have changed, and now remote
In bureaucratic isolation
They have, as authors sadly note,
A self-esteem above their station.
Today they seldom seem to meet
The hard-pressed sources of their worth
Convivially to drink and eat

And bring their manuscripts to birth.
Some writers, running short of bread
Might make a meal of them instead:

A consommé of overtaken firms
Chilled to a jelly and served cold
As bargaining can be as to the frugal terms
On which emasculated volumes should be sold.
Gulyas des lecteurs with a tartar sauce
As piquant as their various caprices
Would constitute the second course
For those who pull good books to pieces.
The *Coq des editeurs*, a caponed bird
Cooked in the heady wine of their conceit
And richly stuffed with every excised word
That justly they would be compelled to eat.
And finally the dish *I'd* savour most—
Some devilled publishers on toast.

HENRY JAMES

LUNCHEON AT BOURG

The well-fed Bressois are surely a good-natured people. I call them well-fed both on general and on particular grounds. Their province has the most savoury aroma, and I found an opportunity to test its reputation. I walked back into the town from the church (there was really nothing to be seen by the way), and as the hour of the midday breakfast had struck, directed my steps to the inn. The *table d'hôte* was going on, and a gracious, bustling, talkative landlady welcomed me. I had an excellent repast – the best repast possible – which consisted simply of boiled eggs and bread and butter. It was the quality of these simple ingredients that made the occasion memorable. The eggs were so good that I am ashamed to say how many of them I consumed. 'La plus belle fille du monde,' as the French proverb says, 'ne peut donner que ce qu'elle a'; and it might seem that an egg which has succeeded in being fresh has done all that can reasonably be expected of it. But there was a bloom of punctuality, so to speak, about these eggs of Bourg, as if it had been the intention of the very hens themselves that they should be promptly served. 'Nous sommes en Bresse, et le beurre n'est pas mauvais,' the landlady said with a sort of dry coquetry, as she placed this article before me. It was the poetry of butter, and I ate a pound or two of it; after which I câme away with a strange mixture of impressions of late gothic sculpture and thick *tartines*.

PAUL JENNINGS

SOME REGIONAL SURPRISES FOR TOURISTS

Regions differ also in their cooks. In Devon is a thick cream (clott) which you may, but in Cornwall more clotted and dispatch to your pal (postal). All regions are something private in specials, and have a rebounding category of cheese; Double Gloucester, Blue Vinny, Station, Wensleydale, Cheddar and Cheshire itself. In Melton, pork pies, in Bakewell a Sweet Tart. You can go all through and find some dash to whet your belly, as Wiltshire Lordy Cake, Welsh Ratbit, Aylesbury Dick. And Scotland Gridle Cake, Stones, Skelters, Auld Leckie and Immortal Hoggis.

And island lapped all round by the sea can pitch to the sky with its fish. It doesn't matter if you have Dover Sole, Herring Pickled, Crab, Tarboy, Puke, Lace, Trite, Salmon or White Bait in a tumbling dish with varnish, or if you want only a snick you may buy Fish and Chips in a Newspaper, it is too fresh the same.

MARK KAHN
also Literary Editor of the *Sunday Mirror*

THE ALL-BRITISH HAMBURGER

Not your plastic hamburger that is served crudely between lumps of soggy flour-mix style bread. Nor the all-American version.

Both these unspeakable horrors belong with hot dogs and like monstrosities. No, the hamburger of which I speak is large, succulent, delicately, affectionately brought to perfection. There were only two places in London that I know of where such could be obtained. One was Isow's in Soho, alas now no more; and Kettner's also in Soho and still very much with us. The Kettner hamburger is made of best beef minced with flour, egg yolk, garlic and herbs. Precisely what herbs, I gather, is not all that important; what matters is that such herbs as you may have to hand are chucked in. Mix all the ingredients together. Shape into rounds and roll in flour. Fry in oil for 10–15 minutes. Serve with fried onions and a fried egg on top.

The late Tommy Wisdom, a distinguished racing and rally driver was also a hamburger addict. I remember many years ago when we had just finished a Monte Carlo rally together going into a renowned establishment in Monte Carlo for a meal. Wisdom studied the menu carefully. 'Do you have hamburger?' he asked. The headwaiter replied with a succinct and somewhat contemptuous 'non'. Wisdom thought carefully. At length, 'You have Steak Tartare?' The headwaiter relaxed, 'But of course.' Said Wisdom simply: 'Fry it!'

We had hamburgers, but they weren't very good.

P. J. KAVANAGH

SOEDARMI

This seems a good opportunity to celebrate Soedarmi, which is not the name of a dish but of a cook. We met her in Djakarta, in Java, and she 'went with' the bungalow. She slept in the garage beneath a picture of the Queen. She spoke no English but smiled and simpered instead. The Embassy official who took us to the bungalow shouted at her and she looked frightened. My wife did not shout at her but bought a dictionary and soon, to our astonishment, we began to be treated to a series of meals that grew progressively more delicious as she learned our tastes and gained in confidence.

She had a stove but preferred to cook on a small charcoal burner in the courtyard, regulating the heat of it by kneeling down, resting her cheek on the ground and blowing sideways. She was perhaps forty years old, small and elegant, and she had been married as a child. Her husband turned up occasionally on his bicycle and then in the morning she would look as though she had been crying. At all other times she smiled except on the days when she prepared *rijstafel* when she began almost to bustle and, having laid it out on the table she would wait with an expression on her face of the watchful attention you might expect to see on a poet as he awaits the verdict of the one critic he respects. She was right, it was a masterpiece. It consisted of perfectly cooked rice, on a separate dish and containing hints of various spices, surrounded by ten or a dozen other dishes of shrimps, dried fish, cucumber and, oh, other things whose name I have forgotten all exquisite, all delicious. She watched the passage of each forkful to my mouth and earnestly scanned my expression for my reaction. After a morning's teaching I found this too much and usually asked her to leave the room. (I go through life with a bag-full of remorses that grows heavier by the year.) Long afterwards she wrote to me – she went to the public scribe and paid him to write to me, wishing me well – so I cannot have been too much to bear. I must have gone afterwards to thank her because I found her in the courtyard sitting on the ground in front of a flower in a jam-jar. Whether she was in prayer or contemplation I could not know. I think she was just looking at it properly.

H. R. F. KEATING

INSPECTOR GHOTE AND THE SWEETMEAT

One other thing had struck Inspector Ghote as he had thought about the affair before being telephoned in this embarrassing manner by Superintendent Karandikar with the wealthy Mr Desai, the very man the kidnappers were asking for money, sitting lunching behind him. It was something so small as to hardly exist, but should he nevertheless mention it to the superintendent? Or would that be taken as an attempt to retain for himself the major part in the case that the superintendent so plainly thought he was unfitted for?

He wanted to leave it. The notion of that tiger tongue flicking out, laceratingly, was terribly intimidating. And it was only the matter of an impression. But then it was something the superintendent could not know about. And it was quite probable that, however big the search for the waiting ransome-money box, it would fail. And then this one feint lead might be all that lay between the old tailor's little son and brutal death.

'Superintendent Karandikar, sir. There is one thing.'

'Ghote, I want to speak to Mr Desai. Now.'

'Sir, in a conversation I noted this morning I gained the impression that the sum demanded—'

'Inspector, I do not want your impressions.'

Ghote longed to stop. What he had to say concerned, there could be no getting round it, an intimate discussion between Mr Desai and his wife. The manufacturer of Trust-X Tonic would by no means care to think that a mere lowly police inspector had been pondering such intimacies. And yet it might be significant.

He glanced over his shoulder. Mr Desai was fishing in a large silver bowl for a round orangey-brown gulab jamun from the syrup in which it floated. He could hear every word. But the image of the old tailor, battered by defeat, was in Ghote's mind and would not be exorcised.

He turned back to the telephone, lowered his voice and spoke with rapidity and determination.

'Sir, I have heard some talk between Mr Desai and his wife. It made me think that the sum demanded is the very utmost he could pay, and I am asking "How did the kidnappers know that?" Sir, it may be that—'

'Thank you, Inspector. And I have said I wish to talk to Mr Desai.'

'Yes, sir. Very good, Superintendent.'

Ghote turned away from the telephone. The manufacturer of Trust-X had got the fat round gulam jamun into his mouth. He was chewing heartily and at the same time wiping the tips of his fingers on his working lips.

'Superintendent Karandikar would like to speak with you, sahib,' Ghote said.

The sweetmeat the excessively rich Mr Desai was so enjoying deserves all the attention he was giving it. It is fairly simple as regards ingredients, though trickyish to cook. You need ½ lb very finely ground almonds, ½ lb flour, 5 oz yoghurt, 1 teaspoon baking powder, 4 oz butter, 2 cups of sugar melted in 2 cups of water for the syrup.

Work the butter into the almonds and flour, sprinkle on the baking powder and then work in the yoghurt. Let it rest for a quarter of an hour, so that it is easier to roll and then rub your palms with ghee in India or dear old marg in Britain and make the mixture into balls, or more classically, two-inch long sausages. Then deep fry. The jamuns will tend to break. Exercise willpower, and be gentle. The heat to do them at can be ascertained by dropping one jamun in. It should touch the bottom of the pan and then slowly rise to the surface. If it bobs up at once, let the oil cool a bit. Cook to a rich orangey-brown. Put the jamuns in syrup and allow to cool, say overnight.

Or do what, life being what it is, the Indian middle class often do today. Go out and buy some Instant Gulamun Mix. Indian grocers in this country often stock it. Only it is generally made rather on the cheap without the almonds. I suspect that fat Mr Desai had his done with more almond than flour, but he should not have.

LUDOVIC KENNEDY

There are several stories connected with the attempts of foreign restaurateurs to translate their menus into English. A pudding on a menu in Austria was once described as 'Rubber Tart with Chocolate Dog'. Gavin Maxwell in one of his books found 'Balls – Catalonian Style' at the top of a menu in Majorca. But decided, wisely perhaps, not to risk them.

The story I like best concerned my friend, the late James Laver, who, on a visit to southern Italy, read at the bottom of a local menu the letters CIS. He asked the waiter what it was, the waiter replied, 'Ees what 'e says. Ees cheese.'

FRANCIS KING

BROWN BETTY PUDDING

Just as readers sometimes complain of my novels that the most memorable characters are the unpleasant ones, so the most memorable meals in them tend to be the unpleasant ones too. Such a meal is that served by one woman doctor to another in *The Needle.* With its fish-pie, all skin and bones, its soggy sprouts and its mousse, slimy and tasting of raw egg, that, the hostess has to confess, 'Hasn't quite jelled properly', it might have been designed as an emetic for a patient rather than as a treat for a colleague.

I am appreciative of good food, however simple, but pretentious food that fails to live up to its pretensions (as so often in London's King's Road), fills me with horror.

Cooking is my chief relaxation from writing. Once a guest even paid me the dubious compliment: 'You know, you shouldn't have become a writer. You should have opened a restaurant.' I have a number of cookery books, many of which I never consult. My favourite, passed on to me by my mother, is *The Memsahib's Book of Cookery* by Carrie Cutcrewe. I sometimes have difficulty in converting seears and chittacks into imperial measures, with results as disastrous as the meal described above; and the command 'place in the ice cave' also brings me up short. But Miss (or Mrs) Cutcrewe has also led me to some notable successes. I am particularly fond of steamed puddings and here is her recipe for Brown Betty Pudding, one of my favourites:

5 oz flour, 3 oz suet, 2 oz raisins, 2 oz currants, 1 oz sugar, 1 oz peel, 1 egg, 2 tablespoons milk, 2 tablespoons of golden syrup, ½ teaspoon carbonate of soda.

Clean and stalk the currants and stone the raisins. Chop the suet finely and the peel rather coarsely. Sieve together the flour and soda, add the fruit and chopped suet and mix all together. Beat up the egg, add it and the milk and the syrup. Mix these with the rest of the ingredients. Beat the mixture for a few minutes, then put it into a greased mould or basin and cover with a piece of greased paper. Put in a pan with boiling water to come halfway up and steam for two hours. Turn it on to a hot dish and serve with warm golden syrup into which some lemon rind has been grated.

On a recent lecture-tour in Japan, I was surprised to see myself described in one of the English-language newspapers as 'portly novelist, Francis King'. This kind of pudding must be the reason.

MARGARET LANE

OATCAKES FOR A WELSH FARMHOUSE TEA

For many years we made a family habit of spending our spare time in one of the loveliest areas of North Wales. We had a cottage there and friends within easy reach, and one of our greatest pleasures was a half-day trek to any empty farmhouse set in glorious rocky solitude halfway up a mountain. We always called in at the last 'live' farm on the way up, to ask Mrs Jones if she could conveniently give us tea on the way down, and it was this lovely farmhouse tea, served in the best parlour with a Bible on the sideboard, which crowned the day's bliss. It began always with boiled eggs and home-made bread and butter, the bread warm from Mrs Jones's brick oven, the butter churned in her dairy. Then there were scones, oatcakes cooked on an iron griddle, and a delicious confection which I have known nowhere else, but which Mrs Jones made as a matter of course and called Cream Crowdie. This was simply some of her warm, freshly made oatcakes crushed with a rolling-pin and stirred into whipped, clotted or sour cream and eaten with blackberry jam. Childish though it may seem, I still make it from time to time when I am doing a batch of oatcakes, and regard it as a rare delicacy.

Mix 1 lb medium oatmeal; 6 oz fine oatmeal; ½ teaspoon salt and ½ teaspoon of bicarbonate of soda; put 2 oz beef dripping in the centre, pour on a little hot water to soften, and mix to a fairly moist dough. Take a handful, knead it into a round on a board scattered with fine oatmeal, press out gently with your knuckles and pinch round the edge until you had a good round shape. Dust the rolling-pin with fine meal and roll out gently to half-crown thickness about eight inches in diameter. Cut the round into quarters, slip them on to a hot griddle or heavy frying-pan, and cook until the edges curl slightly and the underneath is faintly coloured.

Finish by toasting in a moderate over, Regulo 4 (350°) or under a gentle grill. Dry off for an hour in a cool oven or near the fire and keep in an airtight tin.

ANDRÉ LAUNAY

A TRIFLE ABOUT TRUFFLES

In 1810, a peasant, by name Joseph Talon, living in the district of Vaucluse, found some truffles in a field where he had planted some acorns ten years before. Being a mean and cunning man, he said nothing of this to anyone, but experimented quietly and discovered that wherever oak trees grew in his area truffles were to be found. He started building up a big trade.

As he got old he bragged of his money-making discovery, and another gentleman, August Rousseau, far more honourable and with nothing but his country's prestige at heart, set to work to cultivate the truffle and, at the Universal Exhibition of 1855, presented large specimens, which he had produced by planting acorns in certain types of soil.

Truffles, then already commanding a high price, became the cultivator's dream – and everyone went mad and planted oak trees everywhere in the Provence, Poitou and Perigord districts.

Unfortunately, only time revealed that truffles did not necessarily grow where oak trees grew; they appeared near oak trees, but only when and where they chose. Joseph Talon, rubbing his hands, and August Rousseau, with tears in his eyes, realized that they had just been very lucky with their experiments.

Years of study on the truffle has still not revealed why it grows where it does, or why it fails to grow where it might be expected.

Truffles, when they do grow, are collected between December and March, but not without difficulty, for they are hidden some two or three feet underground. Man, however, has brought in the animal to solve this problem and trained pigs and dogs to do the finding for him – as it is all a question of smelling the truffle out.

Whereas the dog is trained to recognise the smell of the truffle, after which he will happily hunt for it, knowing his reward to be some tasty tit-bit, the pig has to be trained not to eat the truffle when it finds one, having a natural liking for the precious lump.

Farmers who prefer using pigs to dogs find the female of the species has a keener sense of smell, but it may take two years to teach a sow not to gobble up the truffle as soon as it finds it.

On fine winter mornings one can enjoy a walk through the lovely oak forests listening to the happy snorting and grunting of contented sows, occasionally interrupted by the ranting and raging of a poor truffle-hunter, who has not been able to control his beast in time.

Some hunters, who have been at the game all their lives, manage to find the expensive delicacy without using pigs or dogs. By studying the ground around an oak tree and noting the bumps and cracks, they can tell whether truffles are beneath the ground or not. Also a certain type of fly lays its grubs in truffle ground and the sight of a cloud of these flies is a sure indication that money is near at hand.

All this buried treasure, as might be expected, is a magnet to pirates and crooks. Though truffle markets, which are open during the collecting season, are well watched over by officials of the government, and there are strict rules and regulations about type, size and weight of truffles to be sold, the greed of certain people has made them stoop incredibly low.

Truffles are bought fresh from the collector by truffle canners, some by housewives, but these are very much in the minority. When they can, the dishonest collectors add a few lumps of coal to a bag of truffles, or paint lumps of lead black, or stick a number of small truffles together with pins so that they look like a more valuable large truffle. Small stones are also stuck in the cracks to increase the weight.

The honest truffles, sold and bought under strict rules, are sorted into four categories before reaching the general public.

The *whole brosées* – whole brushed truffle, washed and brushed by hand.

The *whole pelées* – whole peeled, washed and peeled, usually used in the preparation of foie gras.

The *morceaux*, pieces of truffles which have been broken in transit or in the collecting.

And *pelures*, which are the peelings of the pelées, mainly used to enrich sauces.

As far as the English consumer is concerned, the truffle may seem to be a bit of a puzzle. Held in the hand, it means nothing, a lump of coal is just as exciting, and even in a dish containing truffles it might not seem very essential, but if there is any uncertainty in the readers' mind as to its worth, a simple experiment can be made by tasting a sauce with truffles, and the same sauce without.

ROSAMOND LEHMANN

ANNA WOODHOUSE'S PIE

This is an extravagant way of doing what is normally a fairly economical meal, but I feel it justifies the extra money spent because it transforms Shepherd's Pie into a really sublime dinner party meal.

Large onion chopped, 2–3 cloves garlic, chopped, 3 tablespoons oil, 1 lb good minced beef or lamb, small tin tomatoes, or ½ lb chopped tomatoes or 1 tablespoon tomato concentrate, ½ pint red or dry white wine, ½ pint appropriate stock, 3 heaped teaspoons cornflour, salt, pepper, parsley, grated rind of half an orange, ½ teaspoon of cinnamon.

Soften the onion and garlic slowly in the oil. Raise heat, add the mince and brown. Mix in tomatoes or concentrate, wine and half the stock. Simmer for 10–15 minutes until the meat is tender. Slake cornflour with half the remaining stock, add to the meat with all the seasonings, parsley and spices. Simmer for 5 minutes. Add remaining stock only if mixture seems dry.

Put mixture in heat-proof dish, top with mashed potato, sprinkle with 2 tablespoons grated Cheddar. Bake 10 minutes at Regulo 6 (400°), and then 45 minutes at Regulo 4 (350°).

PRUE LEITH

GREEN FRUIT SALAD SERVED WITH GINGER SYLLABUB

This is the easiest of puds to do, but amazingly good. Make a fruit salad consisting entirely of green-coloured fruit. It must contain melon (cut in chunks or scooped into marbles). Ideally it would contain melon, chinese gooseberries, apples, grapes and greengages, but even melon and grapes alone are good. It should be covered in a light sugar syrup with a squeeze of lemon in it, and should be chilled.

The ginger syllabub is served instead of cream. Mix together one part ginger marmalade, one part Advocaat and two parts half-whipped thick cream.

ANITA LESLIE

NESSELRODE PUDDING

My family has never been very good on the subject of food. I recall my great aunt Jennie Churchill's story of her early days when striving to be a successful political hostess. Eagerly she instructed her cook in new dishes only to see with horror the soup arriving with the egg-sweet she had invented dumped in it!

My own favourite dish I learned when camping in the Lebanon Mountains – dig a shallow hole in the ground, place in it potatoes in their jackets surrounded by wood, set the wood alight and allow the potatoes to cook slowly in the hot ash. After two, three or four hours they will be soft and have an indescribably delicious flavour of wood ash. But guests need not worry. I do not seek to impose a four-hour wait for potatoes on them; I *do* seek to reduce the bother of preparation however. My triumph in this line is a ten-minute version of Nesslerode Pudding – the sweet it took Louis V's chef two days to prepare with fourteen scullions boiling different saucepans. Having started at a few pages of instructions I work out the recipe thus:

Pour a tin of sweet marron into a bowl. Mix in two cups of well-soaked raisins and sultanas then sprinkle two cups of whole, blanched almonds over the top. Cover with whipped cream and chill for an hour.

DORIS LESLIE

FRISCASSÉE OF CHICKEN

Before the death of my husband, I had a wonderful old diploma cook so I never had to cook a meal. However, once during the cook's holiday when I was unable to find temporary kitchen assistance, I desperately invented what I was pleased to call a 'fricassée of chicken'. When I was later asked to provide a recipe for some well deserved charity, basking in the company of famous and exalted personages headed by H.R.H. the Duke of Edinburgh, I dared to submit my recipe for fricassée but omitted the vital extra of a *large cupful* of sherry!

Whether it was published with this omission I cannot now remember, but I did offer it to my husband who, with kindly if fictitious enthusiasm declared it as good as anything he had eaten at the Ritz . . . I think that in this ultimate concoction I *had* laced it with liberal sherry.

Encouraged by my husband's well-meant and implausible appreciation, I gave the remains of the fricassée to two of my prize-winning bulldogs now, also gone before, and, I hope, in the celestial kennels enjoying the memory of my one and only culinary effort.

To enjoy this unique delight, make a roux for a sauce, and gently add the broth of a well-boiled chicken together with a large tea-cupful of sherry, cut off the joints and fleshy parts of the chicken and pour over the sauce, heat it all up again and serve with asparagus if possible.

PETER LEWIS
Also Literary Editor of the *Daily Mail*

OMELETTE SOMERSET MAUGHAM

Omelette Arnold Bennett has long been a favourite literary flavour of mind, though, like its creator, it appeals to the plebeian in me. Instead of the smoked haddock, it is quite easy to give the dish a touch of (apparent) class by substituting smoked salmon. Smoked salmon! At millionaire prices! No. You go to a good shop (e.g. Jacksons, Piccadilly) and ask for their off-cuts, which they will usually sell for a comparative song. Any ropey-looking ends will do because you cut them up with scissors anyway. Then chuck into the omelette along with chopped chives and a teaspoonful of cream. My wife, who introduced me to this, says ¼ oz of salmon is enough, the rest will do for sandwiches. My contribution is to tend the chives, which means giving them a haircut once or twice a year.

I also chose the name to fit the slightly spurious man-of-the-world sophistication of the dish.

GRAHAM LORD
also Literary Editor of the *Sunday Express*

MALE CHAUVINIST PIG CHOPS RATATOUILLE

5 pork chops
½ pint stock
½ oz flour
salt and pepper
2 ozs butter
1 green pepper (de-seeded)
12 button onions (peeled)
1 crushed clove of garlic
juice of 1 lemon
¼ lb button mushrooms
4 tomatoes (peeled)
parsley for garnish

Grill chops till tender. Meanwhile, thicken stock with the flour and season. Melt the butter in pan, add onion, garlic, sliced pepper, lemon juice and simmer 15 minutes. Add mushrooms and tomatoes and simmer a further 5 minutes. Put ratatouille in a casserole, arrange chops on top, glaze with the sauce. Garnish with parsley. Serve with creamed potatoes or rice and a green vegetable.
(*Serves 5*)

GAVIN LYALL

CHINESE CRAB SOUP

Since I gave up work (and thus lunching out) to become an author, I've become gradually more fascinated with cooking. Freeze-dried curries have given way to my own private spice rack from which I grind my own curry powder, and I'll use half a gallon of petrol searching for tomatoes 2p cheaper than at the place just up the road.

Cooking is a great time for plotting; you can't think of gunfights behind a desk. But striding about a kitchen waving a big knife, muttering 'Marinade for half an hour . . . Supposing I made that mercenary a Russian and not an American? . . . Who the hell used up all the ginger root? . . . Try it if you like, chum, but I'm an expert with any sort of knife . . .' – at the end of it all you have something edible as well as readable, preferably but not always separate.

The cats think I'm barmy. They don't mind me talking to *them*, but chattering to an imaginary enemy sends them cowering into a corner making 999 noises.

My favourite field is Chinese cookery, and this is a lovely rich soup for anybody ready to spring a few bob on some crab (frozen is fine and almost certainly more economical than fresh or tinned).

For four people: Up to ½ lb crab meat (cooked of course), 2 or 3 tomatoes, coarsley chopped, 2 or so spring onions, chopped, and including most of the green stem, 2 tablespoons sherry or dry vermouth, 2 tablespoons vinegar, up to 1 tablespoon soy sauce, a pinch of powdered or grated ginger, salt, 2 pints of weak chicken stock (don't waste real rich stuff), 1 beaten egg.

Sauté the tomatoes, ginger and onions for 5 minutes in a little vegetable oil. Heat stock to near boiling. Add everything to the stock except the egg and simmer for a further 5 minutes. Pour the beaten egg in over a fork so that it spreads out in little shreds.

That's it. Enrich, if you want to, with more crab and/or another egg.

WOLF MANKOWITZ

MY SON GERED'S PHOTOGENIC PIE

5 large potatoes – sliced *very* thinly
3 medium onions – sliced very thinly
½ lb button mushrooms – cut in half
Large tin tomatoes – sliced lengthways
1 lb strong Cheddar cheese – grated
Sprinkling of Parmesan cheese – grated
Tablespoon of tomato purée
Tablespoon of Heinz tomato ketchup
Salt, pepper, mixed herbs, a little sunflower oil

Wipe the inside of a medium casserole dish with the oil and line the sides and bottom of the dish with sliced potatoes. Then put a layer of onions, followed by a layer of Cheddar cheese, salt, pepper and herbs. Repeat. Put the tomatoes and mushrooms on to the second layer of cheese, sprinkle on a little more cheese, then another layer of potatoes and onions, finishing with an open potato/cheese layer. Sprinkle on the Parmesan and a few more herbs. Put the purée and ketchup into a cup and make up to half with cold water. Stir until smooth, and with a spoon criss-cross the top of the pie with the liquid. Bake at Regulo 4 (350°) for three hours, or if in a hurry for 1½ hours at Regulo 7 (425°), making sure it doesn't burn. It should just be catching on top. You can add leeks, courgettes, and it's very nice served with tinned petit pois.

OLIVIA MANNING

BARBECUE LAMB

This recipe calls for a number of ingredients and a little trouble but should turn a leg of frozen lamb into a dish as tender and as rich in flavour as Pekin Duck.

Rub powdered mustard, powdered ginger, salt and freshly-ground pepper into a leg of lamb. Split the garlic and stick into cuts in lean part of meat. Dredge meat with flour and roast in a hot oven Regulo 6 or 7 (450°) for 30 minutes.

Prepare a basting sauce of 2 tablespoons sugar, 1 tablespoon vinegar, a dash each of Worcester sauce, mushroom ketchup, brown sauce and cayenne and add a sliced onion, 2 cloves of garlic crushed with salt and 1 oz melted butter.

When the lamb has roasted for 30 minutes, pour on sauce and start basting. Cook until meat is tender and of a 'crumbling' consistency. Watch that liquid does not dry and add water or vegetable stock as required. Gravy should be rich and brown. It may be strained over meat, but if served separately, extra liquid may be added.

FRANK MARCUS

SPAGHETTI CARBONARA

My last attempt to cook for myself was in 1948, when I tried to fry an egg. I left the egg in the frying-pan and returned to my typewriter, becoming engrossed in my work. About half an hour later a 'ping' sound issued from the kitchen. I rushed to the frying-pan but found it empty. I looked everywhere for that egg, even in the drawers of the kitchen cabinet. At last I noticed a tiny black spot on the ceiling above the frying-pan. I suppose that the egg must have exploded. I haven't tried to cook anything since then but I wish I could cope with Spaghetti Carbonara which brings back childhood memories. My sister and I used to eat it sitting under the nursery table, with a blanket hung over it to make it like a tent. As my father was often away on business, my mother frequently joined us.

Cut up some bacon or ham into small pieces (two rashers per person) and fry until crisp. Keep it hot.

Into a large, warm dish, break one egg yolk per person and beat. When the spaghetti is ready, strain and add to the yolks, turning all the while. Add the bacon or ham, an ounce of butter for each helping, a little single cream if you like, salt and *lots* of freshly ground black pepper. Serve immediately with grated Parmesan cheese.

NGAIO MARSH

CHAUD-FROID OF POULTRY

Line the bottom of pan with white of leeks, sliced onions, some pieces of pork crackling and a bouquet garni. Put the fowl on top of these and add a pint and a quarter of water or stock. Cook for about an hour, gently. Remove bird, take off the basting strips, set it aside to get cold. Strain the liquor. In a warmed earthenware dish blend some flour with an ounce of butter, and add slowly to the strained stock. Add eight to ten ounces of fresh cream and reduce to a smooth sauce. When really velvety add an egg yolk, salt and pepper. Put aside to cool. Skin fowl and cut into a dozen pieces. Soak in cooled sauce, which will be very thick but still liquid; be sure that pieces are well blanketed with it. Put on wire tray in refrigerator. Prepare separate jelly by soaking in cold water half an ounce of gelatine. Put one egg white in the saucepan, add gelatine and chicken stock. Mix, strain, and leave to thicken. Pour it over a dish, to cover in a quarter-inch layer. On this lay the now frozen pieces of chicken. Pour over remainder of semi-set jelly and replace to freeze again.

ARTHUR MARSHALL

SHEPHERD'S PIE

What I really like are dishes that have started life as something else. I don't really care for huge slogs of meat and in America the vast T-bone steaks turn my stomach on sight. I like, well enough, roast beef and Yorkshire Pudding but oh how much better is SHEPHERD'S PIE – cold beef minced up with an onion, moistened with good gravy, covered with creamy mashed potato and popped into the over at about Regulo 5 (375°) for 45 minutes or so. It's particularly good when marrows are in season and you can have them as a vegetable covered with an ordinary white sauce. And by the way, if you're turning cold lamb into shepherd's pie, mince in with it, in addition to the onion, a small tin of corned beef, which greatly improves the flavour and livens the whole thing up no end. Heavens, I'm dribbling already!

RUTH MARTIN

MISS CRAIG'S APPLE SAUCE

It is some years since I went to Wethersfield Hall in Essex to interview cookery-writer Elizabeth Craig, but the occasion remains memorable because she taught me how to improve my favourite dish – roast pork and all the trimmings.

The October day was hot and sunny, and she would have been fully justified in taking the easy way out and serving a salad for lunch. Instead, a tantalising smell of roasting meat wafted from her kitchen.

'When you've come such a long journey,' Miss Craig said, 'you want good, satisfying food, so I haven't prepared any fancy dishes – just some lovely local pork, our own beans and potatoes, strawberries deep-frozen fresh from the garden, and some ice-cream.'

Nothing could have been more to my taste, especially since the apple-sauce which accompanied that luscious pork was better than any I'd ever tasted. I told her so, and she replied:

'The English don't know how to make apple-sauce – they just *stew* apples. I use three large apples, sliced; a chopped shallot; a dessertspoon each of butter and caster sugar; a tablespoon of sherry; salt and pepper to taste. Never add water. Just let them all cook very gently together.'

I've made mine that way ever since.

DERWENT MAY
Also Literary Editor of *The Listener*

POMMES ARTHUR

I eat best at home. What about soup made from cucumbers pickled in the barrel; Polish beef paupiettes with *pommes Arthur* and mange-touts (I know a French restaurant which says '*Le patron mange tout ici*') and Charlotte Malakoff? But I can also make supper happily of a thick tomato sandwich (my sister liked those as much as me, when we were children, but she always thought they were better if she sat on them first).

To make *pommes Arthur*, roll 2 lb of damp, peeled potatoes of an even size – either small potatoes, or large ones cut up – in 2 tablespoons of breadcrumbs and 1 teaspoon of salt. Put them in a pan, dot with butter and bake for an hour at Regulo 6 (400°). This will be enough for about six people.

NORRIS McWHIRTER

ROCK LOBSTER PROVENÇAL

Rock Lobster is the favourite dish of the only man in the world who has dined out 38,000 times. He is Fred E. Mayel, the Chicago restaurant grader. If it is good enough for his jaded palate it's good enough for my unjaded palate. His (our) favourite dish can be enhanced even further by using this recipe from Provence. It's based on an assumption of 4 lb worth of lobster:

Finely chop 2 medium onions, a large carrot and the white of a leek. Heat in 4 tablespoons of butter with a clove. Add a tablespoon of flour, a cup of white wine and a cup of stock to make a thinnish sauce. Shake into the sauce lots of parsley, some fennel, basil, salt, pepper and a pinch of tumeric. Crush 4 cloves of garlic and add these to the sauce together with 4 tablespoons of tomato purée. Add the lobster, broken into pieces. Cover the pan and cook gently for an hour.

YEHUDI MENUHIN

GSTAAD MUESLI

Summer is one of our few opportunities for entertaining friends and family: for the rest of the year we never stay in one place long enough to be able to do so. In one year my concert schedule may take me to over a hundred cities and necessitate as many journeys by air. In Gstaad our children and their families come to see us.

With all this coming and going – family friends and colleagues – breakfast should be tranquil, small and private and this is easy if it is begun sufficiently early, and a large bowl of muesli is made up every morning from which people can help themselves.

You need to soak 1½ tablespoons of rolled oats in just enough water to cover them, overnight if possible. To this you add about 8 fl oz of natural yoghurt, a quantity of soft fruit mashed to a pulp (use a potato masher for this!) – and keep a small amount of the fruit whole for inclusion at the end – lemon juice to taste, a tablespoon of almond purée, 2 tablespoons of whipped single cream, 2 grated Granny Smith apples (unpeeled); a grated peach and a little honey to taste. You could add a small quantity of ground nuts if you wished, but on no account should you add sultanas and raisins the way commercial manufacturers of muesli do.

MICHAEL MOORCOCK

LETTUCE SOUP

Being a migraine sufferer there are certain things I can't eat – I'm particularly fond of Stilton and port after dinner but both are virtually lethal. A simple meal I *can* enjoy is lettuce soup, followed by Welsh Rarebit (when I dare) made with mustard and Guinness. I usually play the lettuce soup by ear but here is a rough guide:

Chop an onion finely and shake gently in some butter in a large pan over a low heat until the onion is soft. Wash and dry a large lettuce and disgard any unpleasant leaves. Shred the lettuce with a sharp knife and add to the onion. Stir about a while and then add a pint of chicken stock. Cover the pan tightly and simmer for 10 minutes or so. Allow to cool and then, if possible, blend the mixture in an electric blender. Add a small carton of single cream and salt and pepper to taste – sometimes a little sugar too.

Chill and serve with a further trickle of cream or re-heat and serve with a knob of butter. A sprinkling of chopped parsley looks nice.

JAN MORRIS

BOOK FOOD

At the end of a sentence I call for tea,
At the end of a paragraph, bread and b.
At the end of a page, chip potatoes and hake,
At the end of a chapter, fillet steak.
But ah! when I finish the ultimate line,
When I've brought to fulfilment the grand design,
When I look at the thing and it's mine, all mine,
Then it's Oysters, my lovely with Cold White Wine!

FRANK MUIR

'INSTEAD OF SWEETS . . .'

Keats
'Hyperion'

What has become, one asks both in sorrow and in anger, of the British boiled suet pud?

Remember Agincourt. It has been well established that the medieval Englishman, be he noble or lewd, stood about five feet in height and, because vegetables were not bothered with until the eighteenth century, went to an early grave riddled with scurvy. So from where did he get the energy to win at Agincourt, Crécy and other illustrious battles whose precise dates escape me? From boiled puddings. It is a well-known fact that the Englishman's ability to stuff down boiled puddings was a matter of awe and wonder to continentals. But what chance had the foreign troops, spooning up their hot water with stringy bits of veal floating about in it, against our bowmen, belts bursting with suet and flour and beef?

And remember the British Empire. At its height it was administered by a stream of splendid chaps, light on imagination but strong on team-spirit and decency, who had been brought up on Public School food. Forth they went to far-flung countries coloured red on the atlas, honking with adenoids and, after five years of boiled puddings, constipated to the eyebrows and thus impervious to dysentery. Men who did not *need* to leave their posts.

All gone now, of course. Both the red bits on the map and the puddings. And one wonders whether the disappearance of the latter is not bound up (as it were) with the loss of the former.

What noble treats they were. Spotted Dick: fine, crusty suet pudding studded with squashed flies. Boiled Baby: a heavy, densely-textured pudding boiled in a cloth. It came to a wrinkly point at either end. A characteristic of Boiled Baby was its soft skin – known to aficionados as 'the slime' – which had to be gently scraped off the outside before the hot golden syrup was applied. Even when the slime was scraped off one still had to chase each spoonful round the plate before it would give itself up. And Figgy Duff, the Sailor's Favourite: an inch slice of Figgy Duff weighed about three and a quarter pounds and took nine hours to digest.

They *all* took hours to digest, which was one of their qualities. You could not hurry things after a boiled pud. Nowadays one spoons up a dollop of what seems to be pink-tinted cuckoo-spit and it has no effect on the body whatsoever; one races back to the office or, in the evening, turns on the telly and nothing has changed. After a plate of boiled pudding it was a different matter. One made one's way, with difficulty, to a chair and sank into it. There was a fine, satisfactory tightness about the waistband and a drowsy numbness pleased the senses. In a moment or two the eyelids dropped, the mouth opened and a faint, charming rattle from the uvula proclaimed that sleep was at work knitting up unravelled sleeves of care.

Where, O where – as the poet wrote – are the snores of yesteryear?

NANETTE NEWMAN

BREAKFAST MUFFINS

American Muffins are absolutely delicious for breakfast, or for any other time of the day and for some reason not a lot of people seem to eat them in England. They are so quick and easy to cook that you can actually make them for breakfast and have them straight from the oven. They also deep freeze well.

9 oz wholewheat flour
4 oz brown sugar
2 oz chopped dates or sultanas or raisins
2 oz chopped nuts
3 level teaspoons of baking powder
¼ teaspoon of salt
1 beaten egg
½ pint milk
⅛ pint sunflower oil
Grated rind of one orange or one lemon.

Stir together all dry ingredients in one bowl. In another bowl mix eggs, milk and oil. Add to dry ingredients and mix. Grease 12 muffin or patty tins. Fill almost to the top with the mixture. Put in pre-heated oven Regulo 6 (400°) for 20–25 minutes. Can be eaten hot or cold. Not only are they delicious but they are also very good for you.

PETER NICHOLS

CHEESE SOUFFLÉ

When my wife first got an automatic oven, she scrupulously insisted we leave an enjoyable party early on to be home in time to taste the meal at its best. She'd set it before we left and it would be just right at that moment.

We got home in good time and the meal came on, perfectly cooked – a pair of kippers.

I've always liked kippers but my wife says my favourite food is cheese soufflé. Though not a great eater and never very interested in food, I've always eaten anything I liked. Little and often, like a mole, my wife says.

A cheese soufflé for two needs $\frac{1}{4}$ pint fairly thick white sauce. Add plenty of salt and pepper, 3 egg yolks and at least 4 oz of grated mature Cheddar. Keep stirring until smooth. Whip the egg whites until they are stiff and blend them into the cheese mixture. Pour into a buttered soufflé dish and bake for about 25 minutes in a medium oven.

IAN NORRIE

MAVIS'S EGG THING

It may sound and look like a starter but is, in fact, a substantial main dish which was born of expedience one night when my wife was having a severe attack of unpreparedness, and had to innovate with what was available to assuage my gnawing hunger. Recalling an occasion in a friend's bedsitter when wonderful things were concocted with baked eggs, she settled for boiling them, and produced a dish which has remained a favourite of mine. It went unnamed for months until served to an Australian friend who rhapsodised about it and asked, 'What's it called, Cobber?' With poise, and some aloofness, as though our Antipodean friend had failed to register something as obvious as passion fruit, Madam replied confidently, 'Mavis's Egg Thing'.

Per person, the ingredients are: two hard-boiled eggs, one tomato, half a rasher of bacon, an ounce of button mushrooms (all this is later covered with a garlic sauce).

Cut the bacon into small pieces and fry in its own fat. Set aside. Add a little vegetable oil to the pan, slice and fry the mushrooms, peal and chop tomatoes and add them with the fried bacon. Gently stir them with a wooden spoon over a low heat. Halve the eggs lengthwise and place in a heated dish. Stir the mushroom mixture into a garlic sauce*, re-heat and pour over the eggs. Serve immediately with a green salad.

* The garlic sauce is made with an ordinary white sauce to which is added a crushed clove of garlic at the roux stage.

ROBERT NYE

ABOUT A MENU

The hell with Clio. The girl's a whore. Muse, you do not amuse me. You're a pain in the imagination, less than a bubble in the wine, more than I can bear. I'm glad I never married you.

God damn it all – there are times when a man does not care to fare back further than his last dinner. Worcester, get the boy to fetch the menu from the cook, and you set down what we did tonight at table. That should make war enough for today.

Menu

An olive, stones, inside a warbler;
the warbler in an ortolan;
the ortolan inside a lark;
the lark inside a thrush;
the thrush inside a quail;
the quail, in vine-leaves, in a golden plover;
the plover inside a lapwing;
the lapwing inside a partridge;
the partridge inside a woodcock;
the woodcock inside a teal;
the teal inside a guinea-fowl;
the guinea-fowl, well-larded, inside a duck;
the duck inside a pheasant;
the pheasant inside a goose;
the goose inside a turkey;
the turkey inside a swan;
the swan inside a bustard.

This bird served with onions stuffed with cloves, with carrots, with celery, with coriander seeds, with garlic, for Mr Worcester, Mr Scrope, Mr Hanson, Mr Nanton, Mr Bussard and Fr Brackley.

For the second course of the same

Four yards of clack pudding, London measure;
13 lb of cherries;
Custards;
a dozen wheaten loaves;
two pounds of sweet butter.

For the third course ditto

Twelve apples piping hot and twelve cold pears with sugar candy.

For Sir John Falstaff

Piment, claret, hippocras, Vernage, Greek,
malmsey, Candia, ribolla, rumney, Provence,
Montross, Rivere, muscatel, rosette, Oseye,
Rhenish, Beaune, Saint-Émilion, Chablis,
Épernay, Sézanne, Sain-Pourçain of Auvergne,
NB: No wines of Gascony, which parch the blood.
No wines of Bordeaux, which block the bowels.
No wines of Orleans or Château-Thierry, which fly to
the head. The malmsey is your natural wine from
Madeira, mulled and spiced, and not the concoction
some make to that name – which is mere water,
honey, clary juice, beer grounds and brandy.

PS from the Cook

The butcher wants paying £7 15s 8d.
The taverner wants paying £70 10s 6d.
I want my wages for the last five months.
The undercook wants his flute back, and his marmoset.
There is also the matter of the £13 9s 11d. outstanding from our deliberations with the dice.

MICHAEL PALIN

All I ask for in food is that it doesn't harm me – so any underdone animal is out. A nice piece of red meat could so easily turn nasty – shuddering, twisting, leaping off the plate and going for my neck. So I prefer the more inanimate range of dishes – pork pies, black puddings and the less stroppy cheeses. Whitebait I love, but eat in fear. All those little fishes (a shoal each mouthful) look so deceptively quiet on the plate, but if once inside they were revived by the warmth and the accompanying toast, they could turn my stomach into an enormous internal fishing ground, with all the problems of 200-mile limits that involves.

I find for writing that it is very important to have food which doesn't drip. There's nothing worse than leaving a trail of ratatouille across a freshly typed manuscript – and bits of Hellman's mayonnaise in the typewriter can lose you half a day's work. Cheese is the ideal accompaniment to intense concentration – but it is dangerously similar in shape, size and texture to a rubber. However, my favourite dish, for a really special occasion was, and still is: tinned adder, sliced, fried and thrown lightly in the dustbin.

MOLLY PARKIN

CORNISH MUSSEL QUICHE

This is delicious and can serve two as a main course or four as a starter.

Line an 8 oz flan dish with shortcrust pastry and chill if possible. Scrub the mussels and bring them to the boil and opening in half a glass of white wine mixed with a small, chopped onion. Remove the shells and discard unopened mussels. Arrange the mussels in the flan case.

Strain the cooking liquid through muslin and add it to two eggs beaten with four tablespoons of double cream. Add a handful of chopped parsley and lots of fresh black pepper. Cook at Regulo 7 (425°) for about half an hour.

C. NORTHCOTE PARKINSON

STEAMBOAT

On a round table, laid for a party of about five, there is placed a brass bowl, through the centre of which ascends a brass funnel, through which passes the heat from a burner placed underneath. The bowl has a lid, also pierced by the funnel, and this helps to bring the contents to the boil – the contents being a clear soup. Around this central feature of the table, the actual food, which is mostly raw, is neatly arranged in a circle. There is room here for personal preference, but the eatables will usually include eggs, fish-balls, prawns, vegetables, meat, chicken legs and anything else which can be cooked quickly by boiling. When the meal begins, the host lifts the lid and all those present spear what they like with one of the harpoons provided (some people use a miniature net instead) and submerge it in the boiling soup, into which the host will probably break a few eggs. When cooked, the bits of food are removed and eaten, other bits then taking their place.

All this, the reader will say, is no more or less than a fondue. In the Far East, however, where steamboats ply, there are certain differences. For one thing the guests will use chopsticks with porcelain bowls and spoons. For another, the guests will help themselves to soup when they feel like it. As the liquid is thus removed, the host replaces it with brandy, ensuring that the soup by the end of the meal is really something. As a meal, it is extremely expensive and one may doubt whether many people would want to have it every week. It represents an experience, however, and people are to be pitied who have never had it.

MICHAEL PARKINSON

BERRY TORTE

3 oz plus 1 tablespoon butter, melted
6 oz digestive biscuits
8 oz sugar

1½ lb full fat cream cheese
4 eggs
1 teaspoon lemon juice
2 teaspoons cornflour mixed with 1 tablespoon water
2 teaspoons grated lemon rind
12 oz blackberries or blackcurrants

Pre-heat the oven to moderate Gas Mark 4 (350°). Grease an 8-in round cake tin with a removable bottom with 1 teaspoon butter. In a medium sized mixing-bowl, combine the crushed biscuits, 3 oz sugar and the melted butter with a wooden spoon. Lightly press the crumbs into the buttered pan, covering the bottom and half-way up the sides of the pan evenly.

In a medium sized mixing-bowl, beat the cream cheese with a wooden spoon. Gradually beat the remaining sugar, eggs, lemon juice and half the lemon rind into the cheese, until it is a thick, smooth cream. Pour the cream cheese mixture into the lined cake tin.

Bake in the oven for 35 minutes. Leave the torte to cool and then chill it in the refrigator overnight.

In a medium sized mixing-bowl, combine the berries, water, cornflour mixture and remaining lemon rind. Pour the mixture into a saucepan and cook for 2–3 minutes over moderate heat, stirring once or twice.

Remove the mixture from the heat and leave to cool.

Spread the berry mixture evenly over the torte and serve.

MARY E. PEARCE

WELSHCAKES

I have a nice line in sausage and mash and I'm a dab hand at boiling an egg, a task requiring more skill than many people would have us believe. But I'm utterly lacking in invention, and I often spare a thought for those anonymous brave spirits of the past whose experiments, and perhaps sufferings, led to the discoveries we now take so for granted. Some great recipes were no doubt discovered by accident, but genius itself is an accident.

'Never do today what you can put off until tomorrow' is a useful motto, and no doubt some cave-dwelling dairymaid, finding that the milk had gone sour, delayed giving it to the pig and thus created the first cheese.

Welshcakes are nice. My mother was Welsh and made them often when I was a child. They are more tasty than ordinary scones, and they can be eaten by the score.

You will need 3 oz of butter. Rub this into 8 oz self-raising flour and add 3 oz each brown sugar and currants and a pinch of salt.

Mix in an egg and a little milk (preferably sour milk) to form a firm paste.

Roll the paste out on a floured board, cut into rounds and bake on a lightly-greased griddle over a medium heat until a gentle gold.

LOGAN PEARSALL SMITH

PICNICS: THE IDEAL

Bright shone the morning, and as I waited (They had promised to call for me in their motor) I made for myself an enchanting picture of the day before me, our drive to that forest beyond the dove-blue hills, the ideal beings I should meet there, feasting with them, exquisitely, in the shade of immemorial trees.

And when, in the rainy twilight, I was deposited, soaked, and half-dead with fatigue, out of that open motor, was there nothing inside me but chill and disillusion? If I had dreamed a dream incompatible with the climate and social conditions of these Islands, had I not, out of that very dream and disenchantment, created, like the Platonic Lover, a Platonic and imperishable vision – the ideal Picnic, the Picnic as it might be – the wonderful windless weather, the Watteauish landscape, where a group of mortals talk and feast as they talked and feasted in the Golden Age?

DIANE PEARSON

Writers, by the very nature of their trade, tend to be solitary people (for solitary you can also read, secretive and sly if you have the misfortune to live with one). So although they may pay lip-service to the culinary enjoyment of the Grand Publisher's Lunch ('So proud to have you on the list,' with the avocado, and 'perhaps some revision and cutting' with the coffee and petit fours) what they *really* prefer is a 'little eggy something on a tray' eaten at three in the morning after the successful completion of Chapter Eleven.

I'm told that living with a writer is not all fun. To be woken at three in the morning by the pervading odour of frying sprats is not a pleasant experience, but I was hungry, and so was the cat, and it was all I could find at the time. (I forgot to mention that writers' solitary eating habits are frequently shared by the writer's cat who has all the characteristics of a writer and will happily share a little snack at any hour without forcing you into conversation.)

Sprats, cottage cheese and sweetcorn, buttered toast and Bovril, bacon sandwiches, all are fulfilling experience when you are the only one awake and have the smug satisfaction of a few more thousand words under your belt. But the greatest of these is the humble omelette which, when cooked well, is the prince of mid-night snacks. Very few people can cook an omelette well. I finally learnt from a Hungarian who threw several pounds of old veg-etables into a dirty frying-pan, poured on an egg mixture, stirred it with a grubby fork, and subsequently offered me the best omelette I have ever eaten.

Firstly you melt about one ounce of butter in a really good frying-pan, then put in your mushrooms, or chopped ham, or onions, or tomatoes, or elderly cauliflower, or whatever you are using. Cook it well but don't crisp, then get the fat really hot and pour in three or four eggs which have been beaten well with a fork, not an egg-whisk. Just before you add the eggs to the pan pour a little cold water, plus salt and pepper into the mixture and give a final beat. Then, after a few seconds in the pan, stir it about twice with a fork. And now leave it pulsing until it begins to rise. Loosen round the edges, flip first one side towards the centre, then the other (this flipping bit is very good when you are feeling par-ticularly cheerful). Tilt on to a hot plate and eat. Delicious!

RICHARD PENNINGTON

LUNCHEON AT PONTARLIER

One of the great advantages of living in France of course is that one finds *The Times* with its crossword on every bookstall. There are other benefits, one being the total absence of drinkable water. It is water indeed that separates us from our friends the English, I thought, as I refilled the two glasses with a vin jaune d'Arbois of Louis Cartier after the iced melon that began the more modest of the two lunches offered by the Hôtel de la Poste to the passer through Pontarlier. As yellow, but not as perfumed, as Oncle Theodore's Lavigny which accompanies his fromage de Morbier.

It was probably raining outside all the eating houses of Holborn while the Jurassian sun shone on the vine in the courtyard beyond the curtained window and they brought in the Terrine maison, which, though of such base ingredients as veal, pork, liver and truffles, was so alchemically transubstantiated as to be as distinct from the originals as uranium from pitchblende. Vine and animal had been nourished on the same hillsides, like Lycidas and his poetical friend, and, not far apart in life, they were beautifully undivided after death. It's not only water that lies between us: there's the kitchen stove. And from the kitchen now came a brochet du lac around whose tender flesh, as flowers in a Russian funeral, lay wreaths of onion intertwined with tomato. In the golden mayonnaise piquancy struggled, but genteelly, with the softness of oil and cream. Frustrated pike probably still lingered in the darkness of English canals hoping in vain for such a transfiguration.

I refilled the glasses with the yellow wine, that, falling goldenly into the open glasses, reminded me inevitably of the loose pictures of Danae, especially as the young woman opposite to me . . . But there are – to return to the original thought – other differences dividing us. The young admirer emerging from the Bank with his companion could not so enjoyably have run his appreciative hand down his young lady's spine (most of which was hygienically exposed) had that been Barclay's Bank. Few couples in Piccadilly pause to embrace under the trees – but then there are no trees; or form in cafés and parks an immobile obtuse-headed triangle.

I recalled my wandering thoughts and approached the brochet with the friendliness of one Jurassian to another.

FRANCES PERRY

RHUBARB JELLY

When my brothers and I were children my mother was determined that we should benefit from the natural medicinal properties of rhubarb but this fruit was far from popular with us. She therefore poured a red jelly made half with the juice over the cooked fruit arranged in individual dishes, and decorated each one when cold with ratafia biscuits and whipped cream.

Today my guests enjoy the clean, refreshing taste of this sweet when I serve it after a particularly rich main course such as pork or goose.

MICHAEL PERTWEE

CHICKEN À LA KIEV

This should *not* be made in the Italian fashion saturated in garlic. It should have no more than a whisper of garlic if any at all.

Choose four leg joints with a good amount of breast attached. Remove the flesh from the bone (you'll need a sharp knife and a great deal of care for this) and flatten each piece.

Mash together 4 oz butter, seasoning, some chopped parsley, the juice of half a lemon and crushed garlic if you must. Spread the mixture on each piece of chicken then parcel up carefully and secure with cotton or cocktail sticks.

Egg and breadcrumb the parcels and fry each piece separately in deep hot oil.

PORK CHOPS WITH SWEET AND SOUR SAUCE

I first became aware of grilled pork chops served in a rather delicious sauce, and developed a special fondness for it, when I was a speaker at a literary dinner, but I am not sure whether it was for the normal reasons. There are some from whom the words of wit and wisdom flow effortlessly forth. I am not one of those fortunate beings and speaking in public means morning sessions before the bathroom mirror and inner turmoil at the time of delivery. Unfortunately speeches take place *after* the meal and the poor victim is in no state to do anything but peck at the food. As soon as the speech is over a ravenous hunger descends.

Alas, the food has all gone, the rest of the company is replete and only the poor guest speaker is in a state of semi-starvation. On this particular occasion a long evening lay ahead and during it I was haunted by memories of those pork chops I had previously rejected. I was obsessed by them; I was sure there had never been such delicious chops, such succulent sauce. I convinced myself that I had missed my favourite food. Then I determined to find the recipe and ever after when I am confronted by this dish I am transported back to that evening. I savour the pangs of hunger; approach the food with such delight that I find it quite delicious. It is said that hunger seasons any dish, Memory too perhaps . . .

Grill four loin chops in a little oil and keep warm.

For sauce, combine 2 tablespoons vinegar, 1 tablespoon sugar, a good teaspoonful of tomato ketchup, 4 tablespoons water, 1¼ teaspoons cornflour and boil together, stirring well until thick and smooth. Add salt and pepper.

Stir in very finely sliced spring onion leaves, a selection of Chinese Pickle which includes ginger and chillies, a little finely sliced celery and the flesh of a red tomato.

Pour the sauce over the chops and serve garnished with watercress. (*Serves 4*).

Absence of ideas for meals

REGINALD POUND

YORKSHIRE RAREBIT

As an addict of savoury dishes, I was quickly won over to Yorkshire Rarebit when it appeared on the menu of the London club of which I have been a member for more than fifty years. Since the Rarebit arrived just after the last war, it is more of a newcomer to the club than I. Here is the chef's own formula:

For two people: 6 oz Cheddar cheese, 2 oz ham or gammon, 1 egg, mustard, salt, pepper, beer.

Either grate or chop the cheese and ham. Place cheese in a Bain Marie until melted with mustard, pepper, beaten egg and beer.

Stir well. Spoon on to shaped croutons and finish under a salamander or grill.

MARGARET POWELL

LOBSTER SOUFFLÉ

I've always enjoyed making soufflés. I feel that making a soufflé is a test of a cook's skill. I am very fond of a lobster soufflé though with the high cost of lobsters now it's a dish I seldom serve.

When I was in domestic service and they were having lobsters for dinner, the fishmonger brought them still alive – I used to hate dropping them into boiling water. If it was too early to cook them I'd put them into a bowl on the floor in the larder. One evening when I went to pick up the bowl I discovered that the largest lobster – large enough to be the father of all lobsters – had disappeared. It took me ages to find him. He'd climbed out of the bowl, scuttled all round the larder floor and hidden himself behind the huge bread-crock. I really felt that having showed such tenacity for life he should have been spared. I was so nervous of him that I used the fire-tongs to pick him up. I'm sure that he looked at me malevolently.

. . . then pour the boiling water out of the kettle into the teapot.

Remove all the meat from a large, cooked lobster and mash well. Melt 1 oz butter in a pan, add ½ oz flour and cook for one minute. Add ¼ pint milk or stock, stir over a gentle heat until it boils, keep stirring for 2–3 minutes.

Add the pounded lobster, a teaspoon anchovy essence, 1 oz breadcrumbs, a gill of cream and seasoning. Mix well then beat in the yolks of 2 eggs, Whip the whites of eggs until they are stiff, then lightly fold into the fish mixture.

Put into a greased soufflé dish, tie a piece of greaseproof paper round the outside to come higher than the top of the dish, and bake at Regulo 6 (425°) for 20–30 minutes. Serve immediately it is cooked. (*Serves 3 or 4.*)

DAVID PRYCE-JONES

Once upon a time there was a contest to see who could serve the most unlikely food. One chef prepared cocks' combs on toast. Another did devilled rats, and a third marinaded pigs' tails and sows' ears. Someone else, for a joke, baked crow pie. The winner contrived a dish that was both hot and cold, sweet and sour, appetising but completely sustaining. I was that man. I have forgotten how the recipe came out, and even what the ingredients were, but each time I sit down to a meal I feel bound to hope that someone will have remembered for me.

MAGNUS PYKE

THE DANGERS OF HORSE-RADISH

Perhaps the strong burning taste of horse-radish saves us from doing ourselves a mischief by eating it, just as the transient vertigo experienced when smoking a strong cigar warns the smoker to desist before he injures himself. Mustard oil, the poisonous principle in horse-radish, contains a mixture of allyl-iso-thiocyanate and beta-phenyl-iso-thiocyanate. The amount of horse-radish which in three hours killed a pig which ate it was of the order of 1 lb – a quantity which few normal people would ever eat. Nevertheless, here is an example of another article of food which is patently poisonous – cattle and horses have died, as well as pigs, from eating both tops and roots – a fact to which no public attention is paid.

JONATHAN RABAN

MACARONI SOMETHING

Working at home all day, I try to eat out in the evenings; so my own cooking is nearly all done at lunchtime. Lunch for me means the period between the weather forecast at 12.55 and the end of 'The World at One' before the signature-tune of *The Archers* starts up. With thirty-fives minutes in which to cook and eat, my repertoire has to be somewhat narrower than Elizabeth David's. I have two staples: sausages and mash (with a couple of egg yolks, cream and lots of black pepper in the mash), and macaroni cheese made with a little something to liven it up. My cooking really has only one thing to be said for it: it makes the shoddiest Indo-Pak joint in Earl's Court seem like the Ritz by comparison. Still, I know an American novelist whose regular lunch consists of fish-fingers on toast; beside him, I suppose I almost scrape into the Elizabeth David class myself.

If you can get hold of some Ricotta cheese, the following macaroni mixture is pretty good but you can substitute cottage cheese without coming to much harm:

Melt a couple of ounces of butter in a large pan and add six ounces of cheese with some salt and pepper. Cook gently to melt the cheese. If it seems a bit dry add a little milk to make a smooth sauce. Take it off the heat and mix in an egg yolk.

Heat up a packet of frozen, chopped spinach, drain it and add it to the cheese sauce. Pour the lot over your cooked macaroni and leave it in the oven at Regulo 4 (350°) for fifteen minutes or so.

ELIZABETH RAY

GOOSEBERRY FOOL

When thinking of favourite dishes I find myself turning away from the richer and more spectacular food that can be delicious, but which is for special occasions, and returning to the simpler food of the nursery – which can be *good*, it wasn't all rice pudding and mince. I have always maintained that there is nothing wrong with nursery food now that we are grown up and able to have a glass of wine with it. However, the dish I have chosen is not one which really calls for a glass of wine, unless it be made from the Muscatel grape which has a particular affinity with gooseberries. A real gooseberry fool should be made with real custard and real cream, and is a dish I never tire of. Perhaps because the gooseberry season is too short.

Take a pound of gooseberries. There is no need to top and tail the fruit for this dish as it is to be puréed and all the extra bits and pieces are sieved out of it. Simply wash and put into a steamer over a saucepan of boiling water until the fruit is soft. Alternatively put the fruit into a covered dish and bake in a moderate oven. These methods seem to concentrate the flavour better than when the fruit is stewed. When soft, sieve the fruit through a Mouli, sweeten to taste, but not too much or the acidity of the fruit will be obscured. One or two dessertspoons of sugar should be enough.

Make the custard by bringing a quarter pint of milk nearly to the boil. Beat an egg with a tablespoonful of sugar, pour a little of the hot milk on to it to mix, then add the rest and stir together. Return to the saucepan and thicken, stirring constantly, over a low heat but don't let it boil or it will curdle. Allow to cool then mix with the cooled gooseberry purée. Whip a quarter pint of cream until thickened but not stiff and fold into the gooseberry mixture. Chill well before serving.

CLAIRE RAYNER

I like food. You've only got to look at me to realise that. I am a Rubens, inadvertently clothed. It is to me one of life's tragedies that this particular sensuous satisfaction should bestow its stigma so inevitably. Does a taste for potatoes, a delight in delicatessen, a passion for pasta have to result in plural chins, undulating bosom, plethoric buttocks? It does, my friends, it does! If the other great sensuous activity was as free with its markers as eating; there would be no need for Mrs Grundy.

With such an attitude it will be clear that to offer an account of a favourite dish is impossible. It is all to do with mood, with time of day, with company. With friend Alpha at lunchtime my favourite dish is – oh, oysters and champagne, but with dear old pal Beta late in the afternoon it is boiled eggs and wholemeal toast cut into fingers, while with cousin Delta at any old time what else but bagels and cream cheese?

So what I'll do is offer my favourite person's favourite recipe at any moment of the day or night.

Take a couple of large potatoes. Peel them. Slice into thin slices. Slice each slice into thin strips. Dry well.

Plunge the pieces into exceedingly hot pure corn oil in a deep pan. Remove after three minutes and drain. Reheat the oil, and again plunge in the potatoes. Remove when golden brown and drain on crumpled kitchen paper.

Meanwhile: Take two eggs. Break them carefully into a heavy pan in which a little butter and oil have been melted. Cook until the white is opaque and the yolk set. Place the potatoes on a plate. Put the eggs on top. Season with salt and pepper.

My husband calls this Lucullan dish eggs and chips, and could live on it forever.

An improved dinner-wagon

HELGE RUBENSTEIN

ORANGE SEMI-FREDDO

The peel of 2 oranges
2 tablespoons orange curaçao
6 eggs
6 oz caster sugar
¼ pint double cream

Soak the finely grated orange peel in the curaçao for a few minutes. Beat the yolks and sugar until they are thick and frothy, and stir in the orange peel and curaçao. Fold in the stiffly beaten egg whites and the lightly whipped cream. Pour into a soufflé dish or glass bowl and freeze.

Serve straight from the freezer.

WILL RUSHTON

HOW TO ROAST LAMB

(9) While Oven warms up - stick unpeeled Spuds in Saucepan with about 2 ins of Cold Water. Bring to boil, turn down Heat - Cook for 5 mins. Drain IMMEDIATELY

(10) PEEL THEM -

Of course, they're hot, you fool! Wrap them in a Tea-Towel. Or that silly hat!

(11) Revolve spuds in Cooking Oil round Joint, coating them. Cut hairy bits off 2 large ONIONS and throw them in as well.

(12) 1½ HOURS TO GO

Pop the lot in Oven Heat down to 350° Elec No 4 Gas

You're looking good:

TA!

(13) ¾ Hour to Go

Turn everything over. Otherwise relax. Roll your Own Woman. Roll a Joint.

(14) 10 mins to go

Start Cooking Frozen Veg, as per Instructions on Packet

(15) Put your Plates in Warming Drawer or in Hot Water in Sink

(16) Remove Joint from Oven.

17 You have forgotten oven glove!
Go back 16 squares
18 Decant Joint, Veg. etc onto Warm Plate and put in Warming Drawer – or Turned-off Oven
19 Don't pour fat down sink. Put it in a bowl – leave a bit in pan for 20
20 Make gravy as per Instructions on Packet – but heave in a glass of red biddy
VINO
21 Serve up in Kitchen. Saves time and Washing-Up.
Remove Onion skins
22 Throw all your Accoutrements into Sink – Leave to Soak in Hot Water and Washing-up Liquid.
23 You have Finished
I beg Your Pardon
24 You have finished

JOHN SAUMAREZ SMITH

Dear National Book League,
Glory be!
Why of all men pick on me?
My views on food are firm and sound:
Greed won't make the world go round.
Apply this then to Men of Letters
(Here I humbly speak of betters):
The Muse malignes if she is starved
But cheers if gourmandising's halved.
Rich dreams of luscious langoustines,
Of truffles, caviar, terrines,
Of soufflés, purées, clotted cream,
Had much best stay in world of dream.
True Fattypuffs just don't write books,
They spend their time befriending cooks;
And authors in grand context meeting
Will rarely notice what they're eating.
Of course to coax the brain to think
There is no substitute for drink—
Here's health to authors, joined, no less,
With National Book League.
John S.S.

PAUL SCOTT

ON COOKING CURRIES

Although it takes only four or five hours, unlike the year or so it takes to write a novel, cooking a curry is rather like cooking a book. There must be time for the actual work and time for the contemplation. You must know the rules and the end to which the means are directed, but there has to be joy and experiment as well as knowledge: a sense, say, of characters (or ingredients) developing; and this is what takes the time. It is as well to fortify oneself with a glass or two of wine, taste the curry frequently and go at it slowly. Unfortunately, costs being what they are, you can't throw a half-cooked curry away as you can throw away the odd chapter or so. When you've finished it curry is like a book, though. You can't eat much of it yourself but get pleasure from the expressions of delight on the faces of the people you've cooked it *for*. Absence of such expressions is like getting a bad press. You just try again, later.

Recipe? Only a few basic rules. Cook the onions first in butter until well sweated. Introduce the meat to the onion as if not certain they'll get on well together. Help them along from time to time with spices and stock and tomato. *Never* use made-up curry powder. And don't forget the twist of lemon peel. Best of all: ask an Indian grocer how to do it and buy the spices he recommends. After that it's trial and, often, error. But fun.

ANNE SCOTT-JAMES

FIELD MUSHROOM SOUP

This is a thin cream soup made with chicken stock and wild mushrooms, which fortunately have become plentiful again all over the country after nearly dying out.

Make a chicken stock with chicken carcases, onion, parsley, thyme, salt, peppercorns, simmered until you have a strong stock, and then strained. Do not make this soup with a stock cube, which will kill the delicate flavour.

Pick as many mushrooms as you can find (or buy the flat kind), skin them (easier than washing) and sauté very very gently in butter for about five minutes. (Do not fry them.) Chop the mushrooms and add to the strained stock, keeping back a few pieces for garnish, and simmer for about half an hour. Purée in a blender. Reheat when wanted and pour into soup cups adding a few chopped mushroom pieces and a spoonful of cream to each cup.

If there is a glut of mushrooms, prepare them in the same way, blend with only a little stock so that you have a thick purée, freeze and use with added stock when wanted. Keeps well for three months.

ALAN SILLITOE

Try this at 2 a.m. as a pick-up during Chapter Seven: black olives (from oil rather than brine), rye bread, Hungarian sausage (or Italian salami) with a couple of tiny glasses of neat vodka.

ANDREW SINCLAIR

SPICED PORK CHOPS

Put the pork chops on a sheet of silver foil and turn up the edges to keep in the juices. Pour over them a liberal amount of runny honey, followed by cider vinegar, mustard, any sort of dark sauce – Worcester, HP, or barbecue. Sprinkle lightly with oregano and put in a medium hot oven for forty-five minutes. This is equally good on chicken.

SIR OSBERT SITWELL

LUNCHEON AT MONTEGUFONI

While we wandered through the high, cool rooms of the great house or, if it were not too hot, along the three sun-baked decks of the garden, Henry would be unpacking an ample luncheon of cold chicken, and Angelo Masti, the peasant in charge, would hurry in with a large, flat, cylindrical cheese, the *pecorino* of the neighbourhood, with a basket of figs and late peaches, tinged with green, and grapes, all still warm from the sun – some of these being of the kind called *fragole*, the small, plump, blue grapes, so different from others in their internal texture, and in their taste, which recalls that of the wood strawberry, that they might be fruit from the planet Mars or Venus – or a huge flask, covered in dry, dusty rushes, of the excellent red wine of the Castle itself. Presently, too, a very strong, pungent scent approaching us indicated that Angelo had just bought a large clothful of white truffles from a boy outside, who had been collecting them in the woods. (The white variety is only found, I believe, in Italy, and most commonly in Piedmont and Tuscany, and round Parma: it is coarser than the black, and, in its capacity to impregnate a dish, more resembles garlic, a fine grating of it on the top of any substance being sufficient.) His wife would cook for us, and send in a dish of rice or macaroni sprinkled with them. And these things to eat and drink would be placed on a table covered with the coarse white linen used by the *contadini*, under a ceiling painted with clouds and flying cupids, holding up in roseate air a coat of arms, a crown and a Cardinal's hat.

ROBERT SKIDELSKY

RUSSIAN CUTLETS

These used to be cooked to perfection (the secret is to keep all the juices in) by an old Russian friend of mine, Natasha Tchermoeff, who lived in Earl's Court when it was still possible to live in Earl's Court. Make them with veal, chicken or beef, but veal is best.

Mince the meat and an equal amount of onion – if possible, mince the meat twice so that it is extra fine. Tear up some bread and soak for half an hour in milk. Squeeze the bread and mix it with the meat and onion, seasoning, some crushed garlic perhaps and an egg. Form the mixture into tiny, thin hamburgers about 1½ in in diameter, cover them with breadcrumbs and fry in butter and oil for six or seven minutes. The great art is to get the juice to stay in, not pour out leaving the balls like stones and you can do this by turning them every thirty seconds for the first couple of minutes. Then turn the heat down and hope for the best.

DODIE SMITH

PROPER STRAWBERRY SHORTCAKE

I can't cook. When I was poor I got my food at cheap restaurants. When I made money I got someone to cook for me. I only wish there had been frozen food when I was young, the kind you cook in plastic bags, without dirtying a sucepan. So, in the circumstances, here is a truly magnificent feat of cooking. I've never made it, of course, but I've certainly enjoyed it often. It is *real* American strawberry shortcake and nothing like the pale imitations most restaurants over there serve.

3 oz butter, 1 lb plain flour, 2 oz sugar, 4 teaspoons baking powder, pinch of salt, nutmeg, 2 egg yolks, ½ pint double cream, 1 lb strawberries, ¼ pint milk.

Pre-heat oven for 15 minutes at Regulo 7 (425°). Sift all the dry ingredients together and work the butter into them until the mixture resembles fine breadcrumbs. Lightly beat the yolks, add to the mixture and begin to blend, adding milk up to just under ¼ pint until the mixture is thick and smooth. Pour into a buttered tin and bake for about 12 minutes – test with a skewer to check that the cake is cooked all the way through. Turn out to cool.

Wash the strawberries, save a few choice berries for decoration, crush the remainder and sweeten to taste, preferably with icing sugar. Cut the cake into two layers and sandwich with the strawberries. Cover with whipped cream and decorate.

SYDNEY SMITH

A WINTER SALAD

Two large potatoes, passed through kitchen sieve,
Unwonted softness to the salad give;
Of mordent mustard, add a single spoon,
Distrust the condiment which bites so soon;

But deem it not, thou man of herbs, a fault,
To add a double quantity of salt:
Three times the spoon with oil of Lucca crown,
And once with vinegar, procured from town;
True flavour needs it, and your poet begs
The pounded yellow of two well-boiled eggs;
Let onion atoms lurk within the bowl,
And scarce suspected, animate the whole;
And lastly, on the flavoured compound toss
A magic teaspoon of anchovy sauce:
Then though green turtle fail, though venison's tough,
And ham and turkey are not boiled enough,
Serenely full, the Epicure may say—
Fate cannot harm me, – I have dined today.

N.B. As this Salad is the result of great experience and reflection, it is hoped young Salad makers will not attempt to make any improvements upon it.

COLIN SPENCER

GARLIC SOUP

The English have a profound suspicion of garlic, certainly if eaten raw the breath will stink, but its medicinal and purgative qualities have been known and used since Ancient Egypt up to the First World War.

Garlic soup is one way of consuming large amounts of garlic without the possibility of friends reeling away from you in disgust. There is another theory that if you habitually consume the sacred herb your body adjusts to it and the aroma is eliminated. Lately, garlic has risen in price, if you have an addiction to it as I have, it is well worth buying several bunches on trips to the Mediterranean and bringing them back through Customs; they consider it bizarre and not quite Anglo-Saxon, but they will not go as far as checking your passport again.

Most cooks when they consider making this soup are put off by the chore of peeling a hundred cloves. But there are two ways of getting around this. The first method, is to pour boiling water over the cloves and after a minute the papery skin will easily peel away; the same principle as for peeling tomatoes. Keep the water, for the moment garlic touches anything some of that distinct flavour will be imparted; this water can be used in the soup. Secondly, as this is useful if one has a large bunch of tiny cloves, simply cut the base and the top off each head, rub away the skin that will easily fall off between the fingers; place the cloves into a blender, add a pint of water and liquidise for a minute or two. The papery skin will have distintegrated in the water and after cooking will not be discernible to the palate.

For the soup you need two or three heads of garlic (about 100 cloves), three tablespoons of good olive oil, two egg yolks, salt and pepper. Whatever method you use of extracting the cloves, a third or half of that hundred must first be sautéd in the olive oil for a few minutes, but over a gentle heat so that they do not brown. Then add either the liquidised garlic water or plain water – about 2½ pints in all – then the seasoning. Leave to simmer for about an hour. When it is cool put all the soup into the blender and liquidise, it will then turn into a white creamy stock.

Break two egg yolks into a bowl, reheat the soup and when it is just below boiling, add a little of the soup to the yolks, stirring well; then return the soup and the yolks to the saucepan where it will thicken a little. But be careful not to let the soup boil. It should be served immediately, garnished with croûtons and chopped parsley.

Instead of adding the egg yolks, some people prefer to poach the whole egg in the soup.

HILARY SPURLING

AN OLD ENGLISH MENU

Here is a simple, but elegant, old English menu for people who like to live off the land; Sorrel Soup, followed by cold Rook Pie and Blackberry Fool. The green sorrel soup is pretty to look at and has a subtle flavour, at once bland and slightly bitter, somewhere between lettuce and spinach (indeed you could substitute the leaves of either, if sorrel is hard to come by). Rook Pie is a rarity, presumably the food of kings celebrated in the nursery rhyme 'Sing-a-song-of-Sixpence'; it is not unlike chicken-and-ham pie but with a rather more gamey flavour (again you can easily make do with a boiling fowl or a couple of pigeons if, as is probable, your butcher doesn't stock rooks).

For the soup, take a large handful of young sorrel leaves (dock leaves) wash them well, and stew them for a few minutes in butter with a small chopped onion. Add two diced potatoes and 1½ pints of chicken stock, and simmer for 20 minutes or so till the potatoes are cooked. Now put the soup through a liquidiser or mouli-legumes; season with salt, pepper, nutmeg and a dash of lemon juice; and stir in a cupful of cream before re-heating.

For the pie, take four young rooks but use only the legs and breasts, as the backs are apt to be bitter. Cover them with water and a glass of white wine; add a carrot, a stick of celery, parsley, thyme and a bay leaf; and simmer gently until the rooks are tender. Strip the flesh from the bones as soon as it is cool enough to handle, and slice it into neat pieces. Now take three hard-boiled eggs, quartered, a fat rasher of bacon, diced, and two or three sprigs of parsley, chopped. Fill your pie-dish with rook meat, bacon and eggs in layers, seasoning as you go with salt, pepper, parsley and a blade or two of mace. Meanwhile, simmer the crushed carcases in the cooking liquor, which you reduce by fast boiling until there is just enough to cover the pie filling. Pour this into the dish, close the pie with a pastry lid and bake it in a hot oven, Regulo 6 (400°) until the pastry is cooked. Then turn the heat down to Regulo 4 (350°), cover the pastry with foil or greaseproof paper and cook for another half-hour or so. This pie is good hot, but really excellent cold when the juice will set to a jelly.

As for the fool, make a custard with three egg yolks and half a pint of single cream by warming the cream, adding it little by little to the well beaten yolks, returning the mixture to the pan and thickening it gradually over a low heat, stirring all the time, until it will coat the back of a wooden spoon. Now sweeten the custard, let it cool and add a pound of sieved blackberries. Flavour with powdered cinnamon, lemon juice and more sugar if necessary; and chill the fool well before serving.

JOYCE STRANGER

SECRET TOMATO CHUTNEY

The Hunt came to tea at the end of a day's walking. Came to eat home-baked bread and farm butter, with rum butter and blackberry jelly, and great slices of ham served with lettuce and tomato chutney made from a secret recipe.*

They followed it with slices of apple pie, pastry melting in the mouth, and rich cream from Dolly, the Jersey cow that browsed in the orchard. Lest their hunger were still unappeased, there were also scones the size of saucers and light and fluffy as a summer cloud, and for those with more delicate palates, iced cakes and rock buns and Queen cakes deserving of a poem.

* My own secret recipe makes a very rich and sweet chutney – often secretly eaten by spoonfuls from the jar!

Boil 4 lb of sliced tomatoes with 1½ lb sugar and a little water. Add ½ lb raisins, 3 oz green ginger, rind of half a lime or small lemon, ¼ teaspoon paprika, a tiny piece of chilli, ½ a cup of wine vinegar and a tablespoon of salt. Simmer gently until thick.

NOEL STREATFEILD

FILETS DE BOEUF AUX BANANAS

I have to admit that I am normally a very bad cook. However, I met this dish at a house I was staying in and liked it so much that I wrote it down and practised it at home.

2 lb fillet beef, 2 bananas, 1 small onion, ½ gill cream, 1 egg yolk and a little of each: flour, butter, lard, breadcrumbs, horseradish sauce and chopped parsley.

Remove fat from the meat, cut fillets one inch thick and shape and trim neatly. Beat them out flatter, then fry in a mixture of butter and lard for 8 minutes (make sure the fat is very hot before adding the fillets). Press fillets down as they cook and keep turning them. Put one side in a warm dish.

Peel the bananas and cut into longish pieces but not too thick. Coat the pieces in flour then egg and breadcrumbs and fry. Add prepared bananas to the dish of fillets.

Make an egg sauce by chopping the onion finely and cooking in water for a few minutes. Strain off water and sauté the onion in a little butter. Add the egg yolk and cream. Stir over gentle heat until it thickens, but be careful not to boil it. Add a little horse-radish sauce. Pour his sauce over the fillets and bananas and sprinkle the whole dish with parsley.

PATIENCE STRONG

LIFE IS FOR LIVING

Snobbery of every kind is something I deplore
  Social or intellectual, but what I most abhor
Is the kitchen snob whose life revolves around the rites
  Of cooking and of eating and extolling the delights
Of soufflés, sauces, soups and courses with a foreign tag,
  Seldom does she ever talk of stews and swedes and scrag.
Time-consuming rituals absorb her busy days
  To outdo the Joneses with their Frenchifying ways.

Life's too short for bending over ovens, pots and pans.
  It never did appeal to me for I had other plans,
But eat I must, so give me please a steak and kidney pud
  Stuffed with mushrooms and with herbs. It's British and it's good,
Rich with gravy, and with suet thickly roofed and lined,
  Followed by an apple pie – the Anglo-Saxon kind.
Time is precious so I rarely get this special treat,
  But I thrive and keep alive on fruit and nuts and wheat,
Better than to be a slave within a kitchen pent
  I do not live to eat but eat to live – and am content.

But sometimes on a wintry day there comes a memory
Of childhood's steak and kidney puddings boiling merrily
On the hob in cloth and basin and I can catch once more
The teasing smell that greeted me as I rushed through the door
Saying 'What's for dinner, Mum? Oh good, my favourite.'
Young and hungry, never did I waste or leave a bit.
Enough. Who wants to know? Who'll ever read this little rhyme?
Cook on! But life's for living. Can you really spare the time?

JEAN STUBBS

LEMON MERINGUE PIE

I was born and bred in Lancashire, where both quality and quantity of food are important. (You have to keep out the cold somehow!) All the women in our family were splendid cooks, and each had her speciality, but the *Lemon Meringue Pie* expert was undoubtedly Aunt Mildred. Unlike the others, she refused to divulge her secret, and crowned many supper-parties with this delicious dish – and a Gioconda Smile. One summer afternoon in the 1930s my mother found a recipe for Lemon Meringue Pie in the *Radio Times*, and tried it out on us. The result was so successful that she offered a slice to Aunt Mildred, who said indignantly after the first melting spoonful, 'You've stolen my recipe!' and refused to speak to her for a month afterwards. That little feud, and both ladies, are now laid to rest. But in my personal recipe book, written in my mother's undaunted hand, is the following delicacy – and the best one I have ever tasted.

Pastry: 6 oz plain flour, pinch of salt, 4 oz lard, a little water. Make the pastry and set aside to chill for half an hour in the refrigerator.

Lemon Filling: 2½ oz melted butter, 2 (large) egg yolks, grated rind and juice of 1 large lemon, 1 heaped teaspoon of cornflour, 2 oz caster sugar.

For Meringue: 2 egg whites, 4 oz caster sugar.

Line a 7-in diameter flan tin with the chilled pastry. Bake blind for 8 minutes in oven Regulo 5 (375°). Cool in tin.

Mix the cornflour with the lemon juice, beat the egg yolks with the sugar, and add all these ingredients to the melted butter (which should not be hot). Pour the mixture into its pastry case and bake for 10 minutes at Regulo 3 (325°).

Whisk the egg whites until they 'peak', whisk in one half of the sugar, and fold in the other half with a metal spoon. Pile the meringue on to the flan, making sure the filling is completely covered, and shake over it a little more caster sugar.

Place at the bottom of the oven for 10–15 minutes, Regulo 1 (275°) – (you will notice that the oven is cooling down while you prepare each stage of the pie).

The meringue should be crisp on top, and soft but firm beneath.

MRS R. TEMPLE-WRIGHT

NEVER EAT BAZAAR BREAD

What Bread are we to eat?

Not a difficult question in presidency towns, where there are bakeries in respectable localities and under European management. In Bombay and Calcutta, there are excellent well-managed bakeries with installations of ovens on the latest scientific models. But for up-country stations there is no alternative but *to make your own bread.* It will not interfere with trade, for your baker will be a *rotiwalla* from the bazaar, who will become your own servant, working under your own eye, in your own house, by your own methods. Your flour will come from the steam flour mills, your wheat from the bazaar, your coal or fire-wood too will be purchased in the bazaar. You will raise the status of the *rotiwalla*, teach a most important industry to many, be a benefactor to your friends, and keep your children in health, *by making your own bread.*

The Bakehouse

May have one room or two, according to circumstances, and ought to be somewhere within easy access – next your kitchen would be most suitable, so that baker and cook may feel the force of your presence during your domestic 'rounds'. The oven, must project into the bakehouse, and its door open into the veranda. You will see how much space of the room will be occupied by the oven, and besides this you must allow room enough for the table, trough, two boxes, and other articles necessary in bread-making, and leave ample space for your bakers to work and move about. In the walls have six or eight shelves for your tins, etc. Two small windows, *glazed* and barred, to be left open in the hot weather, and shut in the cold weather. During the winter months the doors of the bakehouse ought to have wadded screens, to keep out all currents of cold air.

The ceiling of the bakehouse must have cotton cloth stretched across, and renewed from time to time. This will not be expensive, as the cloth bags which form the lining of the sacks the flour is sent in from the mills will do very well for this purpose.

The floor of the bakehouse ought to be paved with *pucka* bricks set on edge, and the walls frequently whitewashed.

None of the bakers' belongings should be allowed a place in the bakehouse, and *hookahs* must be particularly prohibited.

Bread Clubs

Ought to exist in every up-country station, exactly in the same way as Mutton Clubs, Book Clubs, etc. The initial expenditure is only a third of what is required to start a Mutton Club.

Rs50 would cover the cost of building the oven and buying the mill. Rs150 would cover the outlay in stores of flour and wages of bakers, etc., for one month, if the club is to supply, say, twenty-five households with bread. A small bakery will pay its own way, a large one will be profitable, and give a good return; and in no case ought any bakery, large or small, to be unsuccessful, if looked after by one lady in the station, or by several in turns.

Get a baker from the bazaar who knows *something* of bread-making, teach him your rules, and he will be very well off on a salary of Rs15, with a mate on Rs6. An intelligent baker, knowing how to make cakes and pastry, would have to be imported from a presidency town on a salary from Rs25 to Rs30, but if your station is a large one, it will certainly be best to get the more qualified man.

Dear ladies, do let me persuade you to have a Bread Club! 'The fate of nations depends on how they are *fed*. No nation can improve, except through the improvement of the nation's *homes*, and these can only be improved *through the instrumentality of women!*'

LESLIE THOMAS

BEGGAR'S CHICKEN

This magnificent dish is served by the Chinese in the Far East. (I've never seen it in a Chinese restaurant anywhere else.) It appears on the table like a muddy football and when cracked open contains the most marvellous chicken I have ever tasted. Here is the recipe hot from the kitchens of the Ming Palace Restaurant, Singapore.

Ingredients: 3 lb fresh chicken, 4 oz dried bamboo shoots, a few dried Chinese mushrooms, 8 oz pork, 2 oz yuanan ham, 1 or 2 large onions.

Marinade: 1 tablespoon soya sauce, 1 tablespoon Chinese wine, 1 teaspoon sugar, black pepper, a few drops of sesame oil.

Finishing Touches: 2 lb ordinary clay and water mixed, dried lotus leaves.

Clean the chicken and dry well. Rub it with salt and marinate. Remove the stems from the mushrooms and soak in water for at least an hour. Dice the ham and pork; shred the bamboo shoots and onion. Fry these ingredients, adding the onion last. Drain the excess oil and stuff into the chicken.

Wrap the chicken in the lotus leaves and completely seal with the mixed clay. Bake in a very hot oven for over an hour then lower the heat and cook for a further 30 minutes.

Serve the chicken on a china dish and break it in the centre with a small hammer. Remove the lotus leaves and slice the chicken.

PETER TINNISWOOD

I like Lancashire hotpot, scouse, dumplings, sage gravy, chitterlings, tripe, German cakes, egg and chips, langoustines, syllabub, treacle pudding, braised hearts in cider, frozen TV dinners, pheasant, bacon and cockle pie and cow heel and carrots.

Sometimes I could polish off all that lot at one sitting.
Sometimes I could exist for three weeks on a packet of Smarties and a whipped cream walnut.
I like Christmas Dinner.

Christmas Dinner with the Brandons
Condensation was streaming off the inside of the kitchen windows and the heat haze made a watery blur round the light bulb.
Sprouts were simmering in a pan on top of the cooker. So were carrots and turnips in a large copper pot, potatoes in a navy-blue enamel pan and bread sauce in a pearl-grey saucepan with a dented handle and a red lid.
The Christmas pudding bubbled in its pot on top of the black-lead range. Alongside in other pots were white sauce, giblet gravy, parsnips and gooseberry sauce.
'Hey up, goosegog sauce,' said Uncle Mort gleefully, and he poked his thumb into the pot.
Mrs Brandon slapped his wrist sharply with a wooden spoon and hustled him and his colleagues out of the kitchen into the back parlour, where the table was already laid out for the Christmas dinner.
'Bloody hell,' said Uncle Mort. 'We're having serviettes. It must be serious.'
The three men drank hot rum and lemon. The smell of goose grew stronger and stronger.
A saucepan lid clattered. The colander clanked against the side of the sink. The knife drawer rattled.
Suddenly the door from the kitchen was thrust open, and the women began to bring in the dishes.
The smell of goose writhed, squirmed and purred round the men's nostrils. Their mouths watered. Their stomachs contracted and curdled.
The sprouts were juicy green and flecked with buttercup yellow. The carrots and turnips rose in a streaming mound of orange ochre from the deep chartreuse green of their bowl.
The giblet gravy gurgled in its boat. The bread sauce heaved and plopped. The butter spread itself in golden, lucent runnels over the light and fluffy boiled potatoes.
And then Mrs Brandon brought in the goose.
It was a large goose. It was enormous.
The men gasped with astonishment.

'Struth,' said Uncle Mort. 'It's halfway to being an ostrich, is that goose.'

'Right, Les, get carving,' said Mrs Brandon. 'Let battle commence.'

MARINA WARNER

TONNO E FAGIOLI

My favourite dishes change frequently. At the moment I like Tonno e Fagioli, because it is easy to make very quickly and can satisfy a number of hungry appetites at the last minute. If the olive oil is good – and it is essential that it should be – the flavours stir memories: of summer, the Mediterranean, Italian landscape.

You can either use fresh French beans and steam them lightly or, better still, use the big waxy, white beans imported from Italy dried and fairly readily available; in this case, soak them overnight then boil them just before use. While the beans are still warm, slice a few spring onions (ordinary onions will do) over them and add the contents of a tin of tunny fish in oil. The proportions should be approximately one pound of beans to 8 oz tunny and, for purists, the tunny can be drained of its own oil and good olive oil substituted.

SYLVIA TOWNSEND WARNER

CHINTZ TURBOT

Fillet a small turbot (halibut will do). Simmer the bones. Cook the fillets slowly in butter and a little milk then put one side in a warmed dish. Make a bechamel sauce using the fish stock; flavour with a little tarragon vinegar. Add to this sauce a good handful of shelled shrimps and, if you can get it, a spot or two of spinach essence to colour the sauce lightly green. Cover the turbot fillets with the sauce and sprinkle with tarragon.

I serve this with an endive salad with a special dressing of two-thirds cream, one-third sherry, freshly ground black pepper and salt.

WILLIAM TREVOR

PUZZLING PORK

I invented this twenty-five years ago and have been using it ever since. It puzzles everyone because they imagine it at first to be *chicken à la king.* It's actually nicer.

Heat ½ lb chopped, lean, roast pork with ½ lb mushrooms, sliced and friend, and about 3 oz carrots cut into matchsticks and boiled. Add 1–1½ pints of bechamel sauce (not too thick) and some seasoning.

Take off the heat and add an egg yolk and some cream. Put into a heated dish, and put some small, heated *vol au vent* cases on top just before eating.

ION TREWIN
Also Literary Editor of *The Times*

SAMPHIRE IN BUTTER

A seasonal, regional dish that requires the minimum of preparation, but provides the maximum pleasure. Samphire is the Norfolk name, but whatever you call it (Pickle Plant in Cumbria, Semper in Northumberland and Sampion in Cheshire) the taste is reminiscent of asparagus, but perhaps that's because the manner of eating is similar. In our west Norfolk village near King's Lynn the samphire man calls once a week from July to the end of August, having picked it from the salt marshes around the Wash (usually in the most inaccessible places). All Sue, my wife, has to do is to wash it thoroughly and then immerse, roots uppermost, in boiling water (don't add salt as there's enough already in the plant) for five minutes. Serve in dish lavishly laced with molten butter. Eat quickly – as samphire cools fast – by drawing the delicious flesh off the stems through your teeth.

MILES TRIPP

YANG CHOW CHOW FAN

By chance I discovered how to get attentive restaurant service and an almost certain guarantee of good food. Some years ago in a Chinese restaurant in Vancouver I was writing in a notebook, jotting down details of décor and furnishing in case I ever needed to use the place as a setting for a story, when the manager came across. He had thought I must be a scout for a good food guide but when he found out that I was a writer he was eager to confess that he too was an author and his book *Selected Chinese Recipes*, was to be published the following day. He left after insisting that I, and the small party with me, should have some special dishes which were being prepared for a Chinese wedding and were not available on the menu. A few minutes later he returned with a copy of the book which he presented with his compliments. I asked him to autograph it.

It was only after I got home that I noticed he had signed Alex Louie but the author's name on the title page was Leon Huang. I was never to know whether Leon Huang was a pseudonym for Alex Louie, or if Alex Louie was the alias of Leon Huang, or if they were two different people. But I did learn that it does you no harm to produce a notebook and make notes, not too discreetly, in any restaurant. The Chinese (or rather, Chinese restaurateurs I have spoken to) have a deep respect for the staple food of their homeland. There is more than one proverb to the effect that each grain of rice represents someone's hard work.

It may not be an exciting dish but, with a bottle of Hock, it makes a good accompaniment to roast chicken or roast pork. Here is a recipe for Fried Rice, or *Yang Chow Chow Fan.*

3 cups cold cooked rice, ½ cup diced chicken, ½ cup green peas, ½ cup small shrimps, 1 cup diced bacon or ham, 2 stalks of diced

green onion, 2 eggs, beaten, $\frac{1}{4}$ cup peanut oil, 1 tablespoon soya sauce, $\frac{1}{2}$ teaspoon salt, $\frac{1}{4}$ teaspoon sugar, $\frac{1}{2}$ teaspoon monosodium glucomate.

Pour oil into frying-pan, heat and sauté meats with onion. Add rice and stir and fry thoroughly. Add sugar and soya sauce and then pour the beaten eggs, with salt, slowly over the rice so that they will coat it but not settle in lumps.

Stir for three minutes. Pour in remaining ingredients, heat thoroughly and serve hot.

And remember:

一粥一飯當知來處不易

'When taking a mouthful of rice, bear in mind that its production is not easy!'

ALISON UTTLEY

MUSHROOMS IN CREAM

When the mushrooms were brought to the kitchen they were peeled at once and the tips cut from their stalks, and then they were put convex side down into a saucer or two of cream. Salt and pepper was sprinkled over them and the saucers were put at once into the hot oven. They were cooked and were ready for the early breakfast. They were poured over hot buttered toast and were a dish 'fit for a king'. We never ate them with bacon, and we never fried them, for then the delicate flavour would be lost. We had mushrooms for tea after an afternoon's picking but they were always cooked in china saucers to retain their flavour. At teatime we ate them with bread and butter straight from the saucers in which they were cooked.

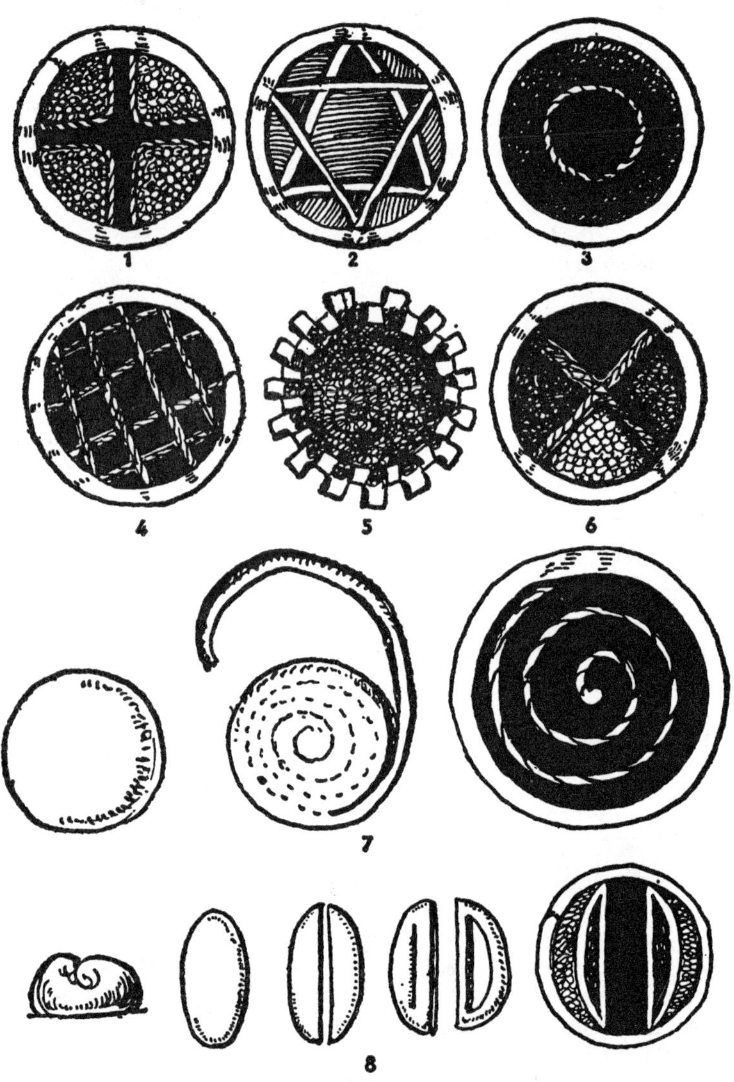

SOME ENGLISH JAM TART DESIGNS

1. Red Cross. 2. The Star. 3. The Well.
4. Lattice. 5. Gable. 6. A Cross Tart.
7. How to cut for a Whorl or Tail.
8. A very small scrap will make a "Slits".

PAMELA VANDYKE PRICE

LOVES, HATES AND A DRESSING

I suppose that I love bread and butter almost better than anything – but only very, very expensive English butter and one hundred per cent wholemeal bread cut so thin that the butter sticks the granules together. Butter should always be put on bread in plaques. Nor should crusts ever be trimmed off decent bread.

'Good nursery food' is always nice – chicken and ham croquettes, cottage pie, baked potatoes in their jackets, kedgeree, cauliflower cheese – but nothing I have to put into my mouth and then take out – like fish stews.

Food that agitated into some complication so that it might as well be crocheted is appalling; hence I am very chary of all kinds of 'cuisine' unless it is superbly done. All that is readly good about traditional English food – *English* note, not Scots, Irish or Welsh – I enjoy. But it must be made at home, with ingredients from a farm or garden, or perhaps moor or stream – gamey game and trout or salmon or turbot.

One thing I absolutely insist on is very garlicky salad dressing made with about five times as much really top olive oil as anyone would think of using – my recipe is six of oil to one of my own vinegar and this also ensures that it will not ruin the claret!

ROSALIND WADE

HASTY EGGS

For each person you need two hard-boiled eggs. Scoop out the yolks and mix with a little curry powder, single cream, salt and sugar to ensure that the taste will not be too harsh. Pile the curried yolks back into the white-halves and arrange in a fireproof dish. Pour over them a cheese sauce and a sprinkling of Parmesan cheese and grill until lightly brown. Serve on a bed of fluffy, boiled rice.

C. V. WEDGEWOOD

FEGATO ALLA VENEZIANA

One of my favourite dishes is *fegato alla veneziana*, provided that it really *is* alla Veneziana which depends basically on the onions. A restaurant which shall be nameless once offered me some large, badly fried liver and when I protested said: 'Sorry, we have no onions!' I am not usually bold enough to send a dish back but I did on this occasion and never darkened their doors again.

I always wanted to do it myself but somehow never got a recipe I could manage – I am not at all a good cook. Then one day my New York publisher took me to dine at a splendid Italian restaurant. He was publishing a cookery book by the restaurateur, Romeo Salta, on the same day as a book of mine. So we two authors fraternised over a superb dinner and exchanged signed copies of our books. I am sure he never read my *Trial of Charles I* but his *Pleasures of Italian Cooking* has been my stand-by for twelve years. This is his recipe for fegato:

Cut the liver into paper-thin slices – I have never been able to do this, I just cut it up as best I can – melt a quarter pound of butter in a skillet; add two cups of finely chopped onion, cover and cook over a low heat until slightly brown and soft. Add the liver and cook over a high heat, stirring constantly. Season with salt and pepper. Transfer to a hot platter. Throw a quarter of a glass of dry white wine and two tablespoonsful of chopped parsley into the skillet; bring to the boil and pour quickly over the liver.

FAY WELDON

IMITATION CASSOULET

I love proper cassoulet as long as someone else cooks it. Here is a method of cheating if you have to cope with it yourself; it serves about six.

Soak 1 lb lentils overnight. Melt some dripping in a big fireproof dish, add about 1 lb streaky bacon, 2 roughly chopped onions and plenty of black pepper. As it cooks, add the lentils, some herbs (nothing too pungent), a couple of crushed cloves of garlic, some sliced pork sausages and, if you have any left-over chicken, that as well. Just cover with water and cook slowly for about 2½ hours.

DENNIS WHEATLEY

DELICIOUS LOBSTER

Lobsters are now difficult and expensive to obtain but they are really excellent when treated in this manner:

Take a large lobster, boil and leave to grow cold. Remove all flesh and throw away the claw shells. Cut up the flesh and mix with one tin of Sturgeon in Tomato (obtainable from Fortnum and Mason), ½ pint cream and ½ pint of brandy. Mix well and replace the two halves of the shell of the lobster's body and serve.

KATHERINE WHITEHORN

RASPBERRY BRÛLÉE

My favourite pudding is one I adapted from something served in a restaurant. As it is heavy on cost, effort and calories only do it for dinner parties, and it's the only dinner party pudding my husband will eat; he says I only have people to dinner in order to justify this pudding and there is much in what he says. It goes as follows:

Raspberries or strawberries (if raspberries, frozen will do) soaked for a few hours in brandy plus sugar. Then make crème brûlée mixture with a pint of cream, 4 egg yolks and a couple of drops of vallia heated very slowly over boiling water (I also scald the cream first, but I have no idea why). This you pour over the raspberries in flat gratin dish and leave to chill. When cool, put it into the freezer for half an hour, get the grill hot, sprinkle sugar evenly over the top and brown it until sugar is a golden brown; it will then set hard as thin butterscotch. Don't take your eye off it while it's under the grill unless you are heavily insured against fire: seconds count.

JOHN WHITLEY
Also Literary Editor of the *Sunday Times*

CHICKEN PLACE FELL

What can William Wordsworth, Samuel Taylor-Coleridge and Kurt Schwitters conceivably have in common? Their good fortune in having ready access to one of England's gastronomic delights, Cumberland Sausage. This great dish bears as little resemblance to common or stodgy sausage as the other great native delicacy, Bolton Black Pudding, does to frozen haggis. Freshly bought in what is now bizarrely re-christened Cumbria it is a pink and juicy serpent of richly flavoured meat, but it quickly becomes exhausted if forced to travel.

Benighted Southerners can only obtain Robson's brand from Paxton and Whitfield's in Jermyn Street; they can, however, disguise its flaccid flavour by using it as a stuffing for Chicken Place Fell – this recipe will feed four plump critics or two starveling poets:

A large roasting chicken (ready dressed), 2 lb unskinned Cumberland sausage (from Clarks of Penrith if possible, otherwise from Robsons), 8 slices smoked bacon, butter, garlic, chives, tarragon, salt, pepper, parsley, 3 tablespoons Scotch whisky, small pot of double cream.

Stuff the chicken with the sausage meat mixed with herbs, seasoning and some butter. Place more butter in a roasting-tin and on the fowl, with cloves and bacon to cover it. Roast in a pre-heated oven at Regulo 8 (450°) for 15 minutes, then for 45 minutes to one hour at Regulo 6 (400°), basting frequently. When nearly ready, pour the whisky over the fowl and flambé. Pour off a quantity of the flambé liquid into a separate pan, return the fowl to the oven. Over a low flame, blend the cream gently into the flambé liquid.

Carve fowl and scoop out the sausage to serve with it in slices, cover with the sauce and chopped parsley and serve.

TED WILLIS

STEAK AND KIDNEY PUDDING

Steak and Kidney Pudding should not be ruined by the inclusion of oysters or other foreign bodies! And there should be a plenitude of gravy. It is best served with cabbage and mashed potatoes. This is a good, plain, moist British pudding:

Line a medium basin with most of 12 oz or so of suet pastry (made with 8 oz self-raising flour, 4 oz shredded suet, salt and cold water), leaving enough pastry to cover the pudding. Slice ¼ lb kidney and cube ¾ lb stewing steak and coat these with seasoned flour. Fill the basin with the meat and a chopped onion and add at least 4 tablespoons of water. Cover the mixture with the pastry lid and seal the edges well by dampening with water. Cover with greaseproof paper or foil and steam over boiling water for some 4 hours.

ANGUS WILSON

LAMPREYS IN BORDELAISE SAUCE

Lampreys are strange primitive fish-like vertebrates with gills, fresh water and akin to eels. The sauce is made from their blood, red Bordeaux wine, stock, shallots, herbs, etc. It is a quite delicious dish. The only disadvantage I know of is that it is at its best in Portugal, which though architecturally splendid is otherwise gastronomically poor. You might be lucky enough, however, to combine it with excellent sucking pig in a Portuguese restaurant. King John is said to have died from overeating lampreys. There must have been more in England in the thirteenth century.

WOODROW WYATT

CHEESE FONDUE WITH TRUFFLES

In the autumn in Italy this is readily available in restaurants. The smell and taste are better than anything else if it is done properly, and the Italian grey truffle put on to the fondue while it is still very hot in front of you. The slices of truffle must be very thin so that they get heated up by the fondue but without losing their shape and texture.

Per person, you need 1 oz butter, 4 oz Gruyère or Emmenthal cheese, seasoning, ⅛ pint dry white wine and a little brandy and a few fresh truffles or half a small tin of truffles.

Butter a little fireproof dish and put in grated cheese, seasoning and wine. Warm it gently over heat or boiling water, stirring occasionally. Add the brandy drop at a time to prevent curdling.

At serving, slice the truffles over the fondue.

WYVERN

A FEW WORDS ON PUDDINGS

Soufflés: The *soufflé* is *par excellence* the kind of sweet that is suited to the cosy home dinner, or party of three or four friends. It is a thing that few men refuse. Sportsmen who, as a rule, shake their heads at creams, trifles, rich jellies, etc., rarely permit a *soufflé* – a tempting, well-made *soufflé* to pass them by without recognition. It is so light, so simple, and attractive, that it cannot 'lie like lead within the bosom': while it cannot but afford a pleasant stepping-stone between the pheasant's wing and the Gorgonzola – or 'twixt the teal and Gruyère.

Jellies: The leading professors of cookery maintain that, in order to achieve the limpidity and brightness which in certain jellies cannot but be considered indespensable, the *chef* must never use a *tinned* utensil. An enamelled stewpan, and a plated, or wooden spoon, are accordingly recommended. In turning out a jelly that has become firmly set, let the cook be perfectly calm. Dip the mould in hot water for a few moments, and the jelly will slip gently out of its prison without a blemish. Ramasàni is wont to use force, and try and eject the jelly by vigorous shaking. Teach him the uselessness of such a course, and the danger that it entails upon the contents of the mould.

Tarts: A tart made with *raw* fruit is far nicer than one composed of *cooked* fruit. Accordingly, when we have an opportunity of making pineapple, peach, and apple tarts with raw fruit, we should cover them for baking without previous stewing. The Bangalore blackberry (called by some a raspberry) makes a capital tart. A coffee-cupful of water should be poured round raw fruit, and plenty of sugar should be dusted over it. It is, of course, a standing English custom to send round custards, cream, or iced-cream, with tarts, and I think it is generally admitted that a cold tart is nicer than a hot one.

Iced Puddings: Here let me observe that we all make a great mistake in putting off the freezing of our ices and iced puddings until dinner is at hand. An iced pudding should be complete in every respect *an hour* before it is required, being buried, of course, in ice till wanted. In this way the possibility of failure is averted, and the ears of the company at dinner are not offended by the annoying sound of the freezing operation which our servants love to carry out as near the dining-room door as possible.

Trifle: A recipe for trifle – that time-honoured, excellent dish, so dear to the hearts of our elderly cousins, and our maiden aunts – will form a fitting termination to this miscellaneous discourse:

Line the bottom of a glass trifle dish with sponge-cakes stuck with blanched sweet almonds: moisten them with sweet wine, or sherry wine with sugar; over these lay a dozen ratafia cakes that have been soaked in noyeau; intersperse (good word!) with these some thin slices of citron and candied orange peel, and distribute over them pieces of preserved apricot, with occasional spoonfuls of raspberry jam and redcurrant jelly. Pour over these a few spoonfuls of liquor of the syllabub. The next layer should consist of tartlet cream, about the thickness of an inch, over which please grate some nutmeg, and likewise strew a little powdered cinnamon, together with a small quantity of lemon-peel, and some powdered loaf sugar. So far, well.

Now take from the sieve upon which it has well drained, as much whipped cream of an excellent stiffness as will cover the dish abundantly.

PEGGY YOUNG

ANDREA'S AUNTY PEG'S GAZPACHO ANDALUCE

For four helpings, you will need:

A 15 oz can of tomatoes or 1 lb fresh tomatoes, 6 spring onions, ½ cucumber, a green pepper, a small clove of garlic, a thick slice of white bread, 4 tablespoons of olive oil, ½ chicken stock cube, salt and fresh ground black pepper, a teaspoon of caster sugar, 2 tablespoons wine vinegar, a tablespoon chopped parsley.

If you are using fresh tomatoes, skin, halve and de-seed them. Trim and chop the spring onions. Peel and chop cucumber. Halve, de-seed and shred pepper. Peel clove of garlic and crush to a purée with a little salt. Trim the crusts from the bread, slice and soak in a little cold water for a few minutes.

Place the vegetables together in a bowl. If canned tomatoes are used, they should be added to the other vegetables at this stage. Add the oil, squeeze out moisture and add bread. Blend these ingredients, half at a time, to a coarse purée in an electric blender, and add the chicken cube at this time. Put the purée in a bowl and add salt and pepper to taste, then the sugar and vinegar. Chill for several hours before serving and sprinkle with chopped parsley.

(Peggy Young is not a famous writer; she just happens to make a most delicious Gazpacho.)

CONTRIBUTORS

Acton, Eliza
Acton, Harold
Allingham, Margery
Anton
Ardizzoni, Edward
Ayrton, Elizabeth

Bainbridge, Beryl
Bedford, Sybille
Benson, E.F.
Bentine, Michael
Billington, Rachel
Biro, Val
Blackwell, Basil
Blake, Quentin
Bonham Carter, Victor
Bowen, John
Brandreth, Gyles
Braybrooke, Neville
Briggs, Desmond
Brillat-Savarin, J.A.
Brophy, Brigid
Brunner, John

Calder-Marshall, Arthur
Calman, Mel
Cameron, James
Campbell, Bruce
Campbell, Patrick
Carne, Lucy
Carr, J.L.
Carrier, Robert
Cartland, Barbara
Collis, John Stewart
Conran, Shirley
Cookson, Catherine
Cooper, Lettice
Cooper, William
Coren, Alan
Costa, Margaret
Cowles, Fleur
Craddock, Fanny
Cronin, A.J.
Curtis, Anthony

Davidson, Lionel
Deighton, Len
Dick, Kay
Dickens, Frank
Dimbleby, Josceline
Dimbleby, Nicholas
Disch, Tom
Dougall, Robert
Driscoll, Peter
Duffy, Maureen
Du Maurier, Daphne
Dunbar, Janet

Elliot, Janice
Evans, Christopher
Evoe (E.V. Lucas)

Farrell, J.G.
Farson, Daniel
Fitzgibbon, Constantine
Forster, Margaret
Foyle, Christina
Freud, Clement
Fry, Christopher

Fulford, Roger
Fuller, Roy

Garnett, David
Gaskell, Mrs
Gerhardie, William
Giovanetti
Gittings, Robert
Gordon, Giles
Gorey, Edward
Graham, Harry
Graham, Winston
Green, Benny
Greene, Graham
Grenfell, Joyce
Grigson, Jane
Grossmith, George and Weeden

Hale, Kathleen
Hamilton, Alex
Handl, Irene
Hartley, Dorothy
Hartridge, Jon
Herriot, James
Hibbert, Christopher
Highsmith, Patricia
Hinde, Thomas
Hiscock, Eric
Holloway, David
Holyroyd, Michael
Hopcraft, Jan
Humphries, Barry

Innes, Hammond
Irving, Laurence

James, Henry
Jennings, Paul

Kahn, Mark
Kavanagh, P.J.
Keating, H.R.F.
Kennedy, Ludovic
King, Francis

Lane, Margaret
Launay, André
Lehmann, Rosamond
Leith, Prue
Leslie, Anita
Leslie, Doris
Lewis, Peter
Lord, Graham
Lyall, Gavin

Mankowitz, Wolf
Manning, Olivia
Marcus, Frank
Marsh, Ngaio
Marshall, Arthur
Martin, John
Martin, Ruth
May, Derwent

McWhirter, Norris
Menuhin, Yehudi
Moorcock, Michael
Morris, Jan
Muir, Frank

Newman, Nanette
Nicholas, Peter
Norrie, Robert
Nye, Robert

Palin, Michael
Parkin, Molly
Parkinson, C. Northcote
Parkinson, Michael
Pearce, Mary E.
Pearsall Smith, Logan
Pearson, Diane
Pennington, Richard
Perry, Frances